MW00638825

A ONE-YEAR PLAN FOR BEGINNING TO KNOW THE SAVIOR

Coming to know a person
is like the careful study of an intricate
and beautiful diamond.
As we see into one facet,
others are illuminated and made clear,
thus, gradually, one facet at a time,
we come to appreciate and love
the whole man.

RICHARD M. EYRE

WHAT

——

MANNER

——

OF MAN

Bookcraft
Salt Lake City, Utah

Library of Congress Catalog Card Number: 79-52229
ISBN 0-88494-377-1

2nd Printing, 1980

Lithographed in the United States of America
PUBLISHERS PRESS
Salt Lake City, Utah

ACKNOWLEDGMENTS

For any insights that this book may contain, I am indebted to other writers whose source material springs from three levels:

Level 1: Matthew, Mark, Luke, and John, whose source was personal contact and direct witness.

Level 2: James E. Talmage, J. Reuben Clark, Jr., and Bruce R. McConkie, whose source was the same, but through the window of latter-day restoration.

Level 3: Writers whose source was the desire of their minds to know, and the capacity of their hearts to receive. Among them: Frederic William Farrar, John Cunningham Geikie, J. R. Dummelow, Harry Emerson Fosdick, Alfred Edersheim, Charles Edward Jefferson, Basil Matthews, and Robert E. Speer.

CONTENTS

1
PROLOGUE

3
POSTSCRIPT

PROLOGUE

Recognizing the Need to Know Christ

Another Sunday afternoon—I am sitting on the stand, observing people as they receive the sacrament of the Lord's Supper. What thoughts are happening behind these faces? Twice a week, one hundred times a year, they partake of these emblems and they covenant "to always remember him." Several silent minutes, one hundred times a year, they promise to remember who he is.

I watch the faces. Some are hard to read, but I can see the thoughts behind some. Some aren't thinking about Jesus Christ at all, and some are thinking the same thing about him that they think every week (a "vain repetition"?). Some (many?) are trying to remember someone they never knew (at least not in this life).

How about *me?* How do *I* use these several sacred moments which are set aside for us to "always remember him"? Do I know enough to remember? If I were remembering my own father twice a week, I'd think of so much—things he said, ways he looked, how he did things—because I *knew* him. I didn't know my father only as words on a page—I knew *him*.

Do I observe the sacrament properly? Do I derive from it the tremendous blessings it is designed to give? I begin to realize that the purpose of the sacrament is the same as the purpose of life: "And this is life eternal, that they might know . . . Jesus Christ." My initial observation had now turned into a worry—a personal worry about me.

I decided that I would study and pray intently *about* our Lord—that I would make the attempt to know him as a great friend. I decided that each Sunday I would remember, and focus, and ponder, and *know* one real *aspect* of who he was. I decided to ponder a new aspect each week for a year with the hope that, by the end of the year, I could begin "to always remember him."

The process of writing this book was a process of striving to think about one new *facet* of the Savior each time I partook

3

of the sacrament. In the spirit of that special covenant time, I found that things *did* come to my mind—special things, some of which can be only suggested through written words. Each of the following forty-eight facets is intended to be a "thought-trigger" to accelerate the mind to the speed where the spirit can take over during the sacrament time.

We are told, by scripture and by symbol, that the sacrament is a time to remember Christ's sacrifice for us. "The body bruised, the lifeblood shed, A sinless ransom for our sake." We are told and retold the same thing through the scriptural sacrament prayers. We are committed to witness unto God that we will keep his commandments and *that we will always remember him.*

As with so much sacred scripture, that last phrase has at least two clear meanings:

1. We will remember and be aware of his hand in all things. (D&C 59:21 tells us that only two things offend God: not obeying his commandments and not confessing his hand in all things.)
2. We will remember his life and teachings and will model our lives after his.

It is the second meaning with which this book deals—the process of starting to *know* him in a real enough way that we begin to have a *friend* to remember.

(We should also realize that remembering his life and teachings is very helpful in remembering his hand in all things.)

My objective, then, has been to start to know Christ in the way he tells us to—as a real and loving brother, a being with body, parts, passions, and certain *qualities* of personality and character:

—Qualities made hard to know because of our differences (his perfection);

—Qualities made easier to know because of our similarities (our common Father and common origins);

4

—Qualities we must try to know because he has asked us to know them and has sent us here for that very purpose (see John 17:3).

You might wonder at the irony of sending someone *away* from you so that they might know you better (as Christ did with us), but is it not true even in this life that "getting away" is often the key to knowing both ourselves and those close to us better? Think of the philosophers and poets of this world, the "Thoreaus" who sought to know themselves by going to their "Walden Ponds," by getting away from those who knew them. And think of the more common experience, wherein true appreciation and "knowing" of parents comes only after we have left home.

I felt that if, in addition to remembering his sacrifice and recommitting my life each week, I could just focus each week on a separate *aspect* of who Christ was and what he was, by the year's end I would have a fifty-two-facet gem of great value—such value that I would perhaps start to know him as my friend.

_____

A small child once found one of his father's complex jigsaw puzzles, spread out the pieces, and started trying to put it together. The father passed through and warned, "You won't be able to do that one, Jimmy. It's a picture of a technical drawing, an engineering plan. You won't know what goes where."

Fifteen minutes later when the father returned, the puzzle was completely put together. His reaction was one of delight mixed with puzzlement: of course his son was smart, but *how* did he do it?

"How, Jim?"

"Well, Dad, I turned the pieces over, and there was a picture of a man on the other side. I just put the man together and turned the puzzle back over, and the plan was together."

The gospel, the commandments, the Church, the Lord's plan can seem large and complicated and "too much" until we learn that knowing Christ *is* knowing the gospel.

The gospel is totally fulfilled and exemplified and focused in him. Unlike any other leader in any other era in any other cause, he was (and is) *all* that he taught.

Scripture captures the deepest goal of life's experience when it tells us that the purpose of life eternal is to *know* God and Jesus Christ. Or is it more important to *love* God, for is not this the "first and great commandment"? Should we be more interested in *knowing* or *loving?* Or is *being* the key—working toward the perfection of *being* like him? John 17:3, Matthew 22:37, and Matthew 5:48 seem to define life's objectives:

to *know* Christ,
to *love* Christ,
to be *like* Christ.

Are there three objectives? or only one? Can we ever *know* him without *loving* him? Can we ever *love* him without the deepest desire to *be more like* him? Can we ever improve and *strive to follow* him without knowing him better and *loving* him more?

The three scriptures are three ways of saying one thing, and that one thing is the most important thing in life.

This is not a book on the miracles of Christ, or on his history, or on his ministry, or even on his teachings and gospel. It is a small but honest attempt to start to *know* his personality and character, to know *him* as he commanded us to, to know him as a person and as a brother. For although he is incomparably superior, he *is* our brother. And though his life and love achieve perfection, he has asked us to live and love as he did.

We know and associate most of history's "great men" with the armies they led, the books they wrote, the wide travels they made, the wealth and splendor of their personal power, or the number of people they employed. But Jesus Christ neither pursued nor accomplished any of these.

Why?

Because he did one thing far more influential and important than all of these: he lived a perfect life. His message, which will never be forgotten and which will never fail, was in who he was. Example is the greatest teacher. *Perfect* example is the *perfect* teacher.

As I think of my closest friends and as I meditate upon the means by which I came to *know* them as well as I do, I realize that it was a piecemeal process. One day (not consciously) I came to appreciate one quality about a friend. Another time I sensed a different aspect of his personality. Then there was the day I learned an additional side of his character.

Our greatest friend has told us that we may know him in a similar way. It can be a building process; each week the partaking of the sacrament can be a time to cut a new facet on the gem of our knowledge of him.

I remember once asking my wife just why it was that one of her friends had been so especially close to her for so long. She said, "I guess because she is with me so much and she is so dependable and predictable."

How well, then, can we come to know Christ, who can *always* be with us, and whose perfection makes him ultimately predictable?

The story is told of a youth who went to his wise bishop with a testimony problem.

"Spiritual things just don't seem *real* to me," he said.

They talked; the bishop probed and finally concluded: "There are 168 hours in a week and you spend at best only the 3 hours while you are in church thinking about spiritual things. I guess that's why temporal things are about 56 times as real to you as spiritual things."

The solution (for that young man and for so many of us) is found in one of the Ten Commandments: "Remember the sabbath day, to keep it holy." (Exodus 20:8.)

Except for the three or four hours we spend in church, too many of us have the same thought pattern on Sunday as on any other day. How much better it would be if the whole day were really the Lord's day!

Too many of us go to church to gain a spirit of worship and love. How much better it would be if we were to *take* that spirit there with us.

Too many of us see Sunday in the negative sense of what the Church tells us *not* to do. How much better it would be if we saw that what we *should* do is to strive toward life's eternal goal of knowing our Savior.

The notion of this book is that Sunday can be a time when thoughts are focused on Jesus Christ—a time, each week, when one facet of the Savior is pondered and prayed upon. One chapter, well-read and well-thought in the early Sabbath, can prepare us to go to church hungry for the sacrament's spiritual food, anxious, in the sacrament's special spirit, to savor and think about a specific segment of our elder brother's perfect character and to recommit our lives to him.

In scripture, every commandment is related to a blessing, every challenge has a promise, every admonition carries a reward. The most eternal, most encompassing commandment/challenge/admonition of all is to know Jesus Christ, and it carries with it the greatest blessings/promises/rewards:

1. That we will have life eternal (John 17:3).
2. That we will be free (John 8:31-32).
3. That we will know Heavenly Father (John 14:7-9).
4. That we will go where he is (John 14:3).
5. That we will be exalted (Matthew 23:12).
6. That his spirit will always be with us (Moroni 4:3; D&C 121:46).
7. That this earth will be ours (Matthew 5:5; D&C 45:58, 56:20).

"But," one might say, "what an effort, what a difficulty to get to know one who is not here!"

Effort? Yes. But not a difficulty. Rather, a joy, a privilege. And he *is* here with us as much as we ask him to be.

Large libraries with extensive religious sections often have thousands of books on Jesus Christ. (In fact, there are hundreds of volumes with the same title: *The Life of Christ*.) Most of these books are written by Catholic or Protestant historian-theologians who, with their many insights and truths, have two universal and common limitations:
1. They draw only from a single source (the New Testament).
2. They deal only with one brief period of the Savior's existence.

In the restored Church of Jesus Christ, we have further sources of added scripture and living prophets. In addition, we know something of our Lord both before his mortal birth and after his mortal death and resurrection. As members of the Church which is under his personal direction we know him through his currently revealed will for us.

I am aware, as you should be, of the danger in *humanizing* Christ. Jesus was not *human* in the mortal sense. We cannot come to know him by comparing our weaknesses with his because he had none. We can come to know him only by the opposite process of comparing our strengths, our hopes, and our possibilities with his. Such a process will inevitably bring about four great benefits:

1. We will know him better.
2. We will know ourselves better.
3. We will realize greater *humility* in viewing our weakness against his greatness.
4. We will realize greater *potential* in viewing his perfection alongside our possibilities.

Ponder for a moment the different levels on which people think of Jesus Christ:

9

Level one: He did not exist. He is a myth.

Level two: He was a trickster, a magician, a deceiver.

Level three: He was a historical figure, but most of what is said about him is fiction or legend rather than history.

Level four: He was a remarkable and powerful teacher.

Level five: He was a charismatic leader and teacher who developed the most beautiful philosophy of life ever devised.

Level six: He was a prophet.

Level seven: He was the greatest of all the prophets.

Level eight: He was more than a man, more than a prophet—he was the Son of God.

Level nine: He was the Son of God and is our Savior. He died and atoned for our sins and was then resurrected.

Level ten: He was the Son of God and is our Savior. He established his church to preserve and spread his gospel.

Level eleven: He was the Son of God and is our Savior. He established his church, but because he had given man free agency he knew that his church would be diluted and destroyed.

Level twelve: He is the divine Savior. His church was established and then lost. Following this apostasy and following the "way-preparing" Reformation, he has restored his complete church and complete gospel back to the earth.

Level thirteen: The divine Savior has restored his church. Through his full gospel, we know him as the Firstborn, the Creator, the God of the Old Testament, the Only Begotten, the Atoning One, the just God who visited and taught in both hemispheres and in the spirit world, the Restorer, the Head of his church today, our Eternal Elder Brother, our Judge.

Not until a person reaches level eight can he be considered a true Christian. From there on, the levels are *consecutive*—each level includes the last and adds to it.

How ironic that the world accepts *its own Creator, its own Savior, its own Judge* on so many different levels.

This book contains twelve sections, each section containing four *facets*. The reader can study one section each month, one facet each Sunday, in preparation for the renewing of his covenants that day. Hopefully such study will help him to go to church hungry for the spiritual food of the sacrament and will help him to ponder, as he partakes, one aspect of the great elder brother whom he is striving to know.

Each month study a section; each week study a facet. In months with five Sundays, repeat the facet which seems most important to you.

Use this book as a one-year plan for beginning to know the Lord Jesus Christ.

As you read, remember:

With the intellect alone we can never discover Him, nor with the mere bodily senses, nor with the teachings of the scriptures; only with the inspiration, the intuition, the sudden flaming illumination of the heart as it happened that day in the soul of Peter: "Blessed art thou, Simon Bar Jonah, for flesh and blood hath not revealed it to you, but my Father which is in heaven" (Giovanni Papini, *Life of Christ*, 1923).

Prayer and scripture are the places to learn of Christ. If this book substitutes for either it fails. If it promotes both, it succeeds.

Bear in mind that the facets of the Savior's personality only help us to know more *about* him (which is different from *knowing* him). His facets are like those of a diamond—only *revealing* and *transmitting* the radiance that shines from within. No facet is sufficient explanation of itself, and no facet possesses the source of its own luster.

11

The source, the light within, will not be found on the pages of any book, but on the pages of your heart.

I emphasize that this is not so much a book to be read as it is a *program* to be followed. It is written to be read one small chapter at a time, one *facet* each Sunday morning before going to church. It is important to read slowly, thoughtfully, and to turn to and read each scripture that each chapter refers to.

Remember, too, that it is not only what you read each Sunday morning that will help you start to know the Savior—it is how you *ponder* that reading later in the day as you partake of the sacrament.

The Savior whom we seek to know is a brother whom we once knew well. The veil is a selective or semi-permeable membrane, blocking thoughts of our first home, but letting through some familiar *feelings*.

Perhaps this book's words will prompt the prayer which prompts those feelings. As you read and as you pray, please remember that what you are trying to do is to *remember*.

12

2
PROGRAM

Meeting the Need

MONTH 1
HIS ROLES

"I am the light and life of the world"

WEEK 1 *EVERY CRUCIAL ROLE*

All true Christians believe that Jesus Christ was the Son of God and the Savior of all mankind. These truths bloom into even greater reality when woven into the organized tapestry of eternity and when knit into the texture of the other roles that Jesus Christ has taken in the Father's eternal plan.

Through his revealed word, we can know the Lord as:

1. A great intelligence prior to his (and our) spiritual creation.
2. The firstborn spirit son of our Heavenly Father.
3. A great and loyal leader in the spirit world.
4. The leading advocate of the plan of agency and redemption for this mortal existence, and the one who insisted that all credit and glory be given to the Father.
5. The accepted volunteer for the supremely difficult and self-sacrificing implementation of that plan of agency and redemption.
6. The creator of this world.
7. The light of this world.
8. Jehovah, the God of the Old Testament.
9. The Only Begotten Son of the Father in the flesh.
10. The only perfect man ever to live.
11. The head of the original Church of Jesus Christ.
12. The teacher of the full gospel ("good news").
13. The Savior and Redeemer of the world who willingly gave his life for us all.
14. The first fruits of a glorious resurrection, which, because of him, will apply to us all.
15. The direct, resurrected teacher of the gospel to his "other sheep"—in the spirit world, in the Americas, to the lost ten tribes.
16. The Mediator with the Father.
17. The restorer of the fullness of his gospel.
18. The Lord who will come again and reign during the Millennium.

19. Our judge.
20. Our father, if we accept him and live his command-
    ments.

Sometimes little children (whom Christ told us to be like)
can say simply what we try to say complexly, as when I asked
my four-year-old daughter:
    "Who is Jesus?"
    "Our brother."
    "Why did he come to earth?"
    "To show us how to love each other and to show us how
it works when we die."
    "What is he doing now?"
    "Taking care of all of us from way up there."

WEEK 2 PRE-EARTH ROLES

Christ has left us with considerable insight concerning his
existence (and ours) prior to this earth. Knowledge of this
pre-earth life provides the basis for answers to questions that
are otherwise unanswerable—the "whys" of justice and
seeming inequality in this world. It also helps us in coming to
know Christ, because we realize that seeking him here on
earth is more analogous to becoming *reacquainted* with an
old friend than to *making* a new one.

The gospel teaches us that we have existed eternally as
intelligences and that, among those intelligences, was one
who was "greater than they all" (perhaps meaning "more
intelligent than all other intelligences combined"). We were
all spiritually begotten by our Heavenly Father, "born" into
a spiritual existence. We were intelligences that became clad
in spiritual bodies, with God as our true and literal father. The
firstborn into this spiritual life was the greatest intelligence
among God's spirit children, even Jesus Christ.

When our wise Father proclaimed the privilege of a
physical body on earth (and when we, knowing the growth

17

we would gain, shouted for joy), the leading advocate of the Father's plan of agency and the leading opponent of Satan's plan of coercion was Jesus Christ. He led and inspired us in that greatest of all eternal causes, the fight for agency, and we followed him as a wise child follows a great elder brother.

Inherent in the Father's plan of agency was the need for an atonement—a ransom for our inevitable mistakes, a ransom that would allow us to *return*. Jesus offered himself, not only to *pay* the price with his death, but to *win* that price with his life—to live with the perfection that would enable him to give his life rather than have it taken.

So it was there that he was foreordained to teach us all, to lead us all, to save us all.

With the plan now prepared and complete (completed partially by the one-third who left in rebellion, providing the opposition that is necessary in all things), Jesus Christ, who was the leading advocate of the plan, became the key to the plan's *implementation:* first, through the creation of this earth, and second, through his perfect life and atoning death.

WEEK **3** EARTH ROLES

It may be that even before Christ was the *life* of this world he was the *light* of this world. The one thing all men have in common is the *light of Christ*—the deep-seated, subconsciously remembered connection of our spirits to his. This light separates right from wrong, inherent good from inherent evil. Some call it conscience, some call it inborn morality, some deny it altogether, but *all* of us have it (at least until it is snuffed out by sustained evil or intentional wickedness).

Jesus Christ is, has always been, and will always be the God of the earth which he created (always with his loyalty to and his direction from his Father and our Father). He was (and is) Jehovah, the God of the Old Testament, who spoke with Moses and Abraham and who gave us the ten items of loving counsel from a wise Father, ten ways to live together successfully and be happy: the Ten Commandments.

Then, in the meridian of time, the God of this world came to live on this world—to take on flesh, to take on the joys and difficulties and choices, and to take upon himself our sins. He came as the literal Son of God, the Only Begotten of the Father.

What did he do during his short lifetime—or, more important, what did he give?

1. The singular example of a perfect life.
2. The answers to life's eternal question of *who* we are.
3. The simple, pure, and revolutionary doctrines of love and charity.
4. The organization of a church to perpetuate and preserve those doctrines.
5. His life for our sins.

But can a list of what Christ gave us really be made? No matter how we think of it, he gave *all* for us. Because of his mortal mother, the Lord possessed the characteristics of a mortal during his earthly lifetime. He was, as we are, subject to pain, to difficulty, to temptation, to the weaknesses of mortal flesh. But because of his immortal father and his perfect existence, Jesus also possessed control over his life and death so that his life could not be taken. It could only be given.

WEEK 4 AFTER-RESURRECTION ROLES

Did the heavens close shortly after the Lord's resurrection? Will not Christ correspond again with the world until his millennial second coming? The "yes they did and no he will not" answers of traditional Christianity are inconsistent with scripture and inconsistent with the reason and faith of a true Christian mind.

The Lord said there were "other sheep" whom he must bring, who must hear his voice. What a joy to know that he organized the teaching of his gospel to those in the spirit world (1 Peter 3:18, 4:6; D&C 138:11-32), to the House of Israel on the Americas (3 Nephi), to the lost ten tribes (3 Nephi 16)! In short, what a joy to know that Jesus' gospel was and is for all men and that he, in his perfect justice, assures that all men of all ages have the chance to choose!

The Lord said to his apostles, "Lo, I am with you alway" (Matthew 28:20). What a joy to know that throughout the two thousand years since his resurrection (just as before) the effectual, fervent prayers of righteous men and women have been answered! What a joy to know that there have been no "dark ages" in terms of the light of Christ—to know that, even in times when an organized church of consistent truth did not exist on earth, individual seekers of truth could still *seek* through prayer and *find* through the answers given by his light!

The Lord said that he would reveal his actions to his prophets (Amos 3:7), and he promised a restoration through divine messengers (Matthew 17:11). What a joy to know that in 1820, following the preparatory work of the Reformers, the Lord saw fit to restore the fullness of his gospel through the vehicle of a living prophet! And what a still greater joy to have his promise that this fullness will remain, protected by living apostles, until he comes again!

The Lord said he would come to usher in the Millennium (see Revelation 1:7). What a joy to know that we are preparing now, striving to prepare the earth for that day of days when he will begin his personal reign of one thousand years!

The Lord said he would judge the nations (John 5:22, 30; 9:39; 2 Timothy 4:1). What a joy (and ultimate comfort) to know that *he*—he who has descended below the depth of our own troubles and temptations, he who framed and implemented the plan and creation of this earth, he who loves us so much that he gave his life for us, he who is and will always be our brother—*he* will be our judge!

MONTH 2
HIS JOY

"Be of good cheer"

WEEK 5 VALLEYS AND PEAKS

A depiction of Christ as a man without joy is as wrong and unreal as a depiction of him without sorrow. He did, in fact, experience the deepest sorrow and pain and grief that any being on this earth has experienced or will ever experience, for he descended below them all (D&C 122:8). But with Christ, as with most of us, the depth of the valleys corresponded to the height of the peaks. There was no conflict between the Lord's happiness and his sorrow. Both came from the same great capacity to *feel*, the same breadth of sensitivity. (The ocean, with enough sweep and depth for great tempests, also has room for sunny calms, with a range and horizon that no small pool can know.) The Lord experienced the height of the Transfiguration and the depth of Gethsemane.

Indeed, it is the clouds that cause the rainbow. And Christ did, in very real fact, experience the greatest joy ever known to a being on this earth. Those who view Christ as consistently sad and somber must find difficulty imagining the Lord voicing his most common greetings: "Be of good cheer" (Acts 23:11; 27:22, 25), and "Be not . . . of a sad countenance" (Matthew 6:16).

It has been said that joy is composed of three key ingredients:

1. Close relationships with God and man, and service to both.
2. A worthy, deeply felt mission or cause in life.
3. Personal health and self-discipline.

If these are true measurements, Christ quickly qualifies as the greatest example of joy.

One has only to read his words to feel his joy. Indeed, his message bears the title of gospel or "good news," and from the angel's first announcement, his life was "good tidings of great joy" (Luke 2:10). That gospel and that life were of such paramount importance that John the Baptist leaped in his mother's womb at the sound of Mary's voice (Luke 1:44).

Rarely did Christ take the time to defend his actions to the Pharisees, and two of those times Christ's defense was in response to their criticism regarding the scope of his relationships with others (Mark 2:18-19, Matthew 9:10-15). He compared himself to the bridegroom and he encouraged the joy of others in his presence. His mode of teaching was positive and joyous.

The Lord lived a perfect life. The perfect life, by definition, must also be the joyous life.

Jesus' love for children, his feelings for the sea and wind, his constantly helpful and positive way, his singleness of purpose—all describe a being of great joy. And well they should, for here was one partaking of and exemplifying the joy which he had made available for man *and* which he had created man to receive.

WEEK 6 HAPPINESS

Storm Jameson, the poet-philosopher, wrote perceptively of happiness:

It is an illusion to think that more comfort brings more happiness. True happiness comes of the capacity to think freely, to feel deeply, to enjoy simply, to risk life, to be needed.

Think for a moment, in this framework, of Jesus Christ:

—whose thought still frees men's minds
—who felt (in both directions) more deeply that any other
—who relished and loved all that was simple and pure
—who actually *gave* his life
—who is needed by every member of the human race.

Edwin Markham wrote of happiness in a slightly lighter vein:

Happiness is a thing of here and now;
The bright leaf in the hand, the moment's sun,

23

The fight accomplished or the summit won.

Joy, in the gospel sense, is more than happiness or pleasure, but it is certainly inclusive of both. The Gospels present a Savior who responded to people, who appreciated men's good humor, who found simple pleasure in everyday life. The scriptures do not tell us of the expression on his face or describe the tone in his voice, but when we consider Christ's supreme inner peace we begin to imagine the happy characteristics he must have exemplified.

The Lord's life often seems to suggest a beautiful and light touch—a good-humored approach to life—like a fresh breeze on the sparkling surface of a deep and mighty sea. Do we detect any humor as such? Certainly there would not be humor in the sarcastic, cynical sense—and never out of derision, where one man's laughter is another man's misfortune or ridicule—but perhaps humor in the lighter, truer sense: the sense of seeing life's little ironies, of appreciating amusing things, of smiling at surprises.

The sparkle of the Savior's outlook comes through in his dramatized object lessons: a mote in one man's eye, a *beam* in that of his critic (see Matthew 7:3); a man who was forgiven a huge debt but who would not himself forgive a small one (see Matthew 18:23-35). His understanding of human nature shows as he tells of the man in bed late at night who is too sleepy to answer his neighbor's knock (see Luke 11:5-8), or of one blind man leading another into the ditch (see Luke 6:39).

Much of Jesus' life was sociable and people-oriented. To him it was appropriate and natural to be at a wedding (see John 2:1-10); dining out by invitation (see Luke 7:36); or simply relaxing in the house of friends (see John 12:1). And how right it is that life's perfect example should exemplify joy—and should take joy in the very things he had created in order that man "might have joy" (2 Nephi 2:25).

The Lord taught that the sacrifices required by the gospel are a joy to make, likening them in parables to the man who in his joy sold all that he had to buy a precious pearl (see Mat-

thew 13:45-46). All of the rewards the Lord promised to those who followed his gospel were related to this principle. He promised:
- —happiness (see John 13:17)
- —joy (see John 16:22; Luke 24:52)
- —peace (see John 16:33)
- —more abundant life (see John 10:10)
- —freedom (see John 8:31-32).

The Savior followed his gospel as perfectly as he taught it: and thus each of these rewards was his to receive as well as to give.

WEEK 7 OPTIMISM AND POSITIVE ATTITUDE

In the Savior's teachings, the wheat prevailed against the tares, the tiny mustard seed grew, the yeast swelled the whole loaf, and optimism abounded (Matthew 13:24-33).

The Savior never doubted his purpose. The possibility of failure never crossed his mind, despite odds that, to mortal eyes, seemed overwhelming.

In the Savior's gospel, all things are stated in the positive: what *to* do instead of what *not to* do, with the overriding positive promise that the sure way of avoiding evil is to be doing good. The gospel is the most positive philosophy of all time, and its author was (and is) the most positive *being* of all time.

His optimism never failed. In his parables we find that the good always wins; in his stories we find the epitome of "the happy ending"; in his life we find a sureness of purpose and an assurance of ultimate success (even at moments so dark that his chosen twelve had fled his side).

Who but this world's most positive and optimistic being could love nature as he did? Who but the world's most positive person would love children as he did (Mark 10:16)? Who

25

but this kind of an optimist would want his disciples (even as he awaited his crucifixion) to have joy (John 15:11), and who would teach them so well that those disciples never forgot? Even after his death, his disciples took food with gladness (Acts 2:46); rejoiced when they suffered shame for his name (Acts 5:41); sang and rejoiced in the jails of Rome (Philippians 4:4, Acts 16:25); and taught that the fruits of the spirit were love, joy, and peace (Galatians 5:22). When Paul dreamed of the departed Master, he dreamed of Him saying to the disciples, "Be of good cheer" (Acts 23:11).

He was the Bridegroom, the bringer of joy, the one who told us to rejoice in the day of persecution for his sake, to leap for joy (Luke 6:23); to look happy even when we are fasting (Matthew 6:16-18); and to be exceedingly glad (Matthew 5:12; also see 2 Nephi 9:18; Job 38:7; Psalms 30:5; Isaiah 35:10; Matthew 13:20; 2 Corinthians 2:3; Hebrews 12:2; and 1 Peter 1:8). It was he who revealed to Lehi that "men are, that they might have joy" (2 Nephi 2:25).

WEEK 8 GRATITUDE

How closely (perfectly?) gratitude equates with joy! Gratitude is joy. Awareness and appreciation are joy. Joy is gratitude and awareness and appreciation. Accomplishments, knowledge, even beliefs make us happy only as we respond to them with *gratitude*.

Our Savior's whole life so brimmed with gratitude to his Father that it often flowed over. The two great seventeenth chapters (John 17 and 3 Nephi 17) are filled with acknowledgment of God and with thanksgiving. He gave thanks for bread (Mark 8:6, John 6:11) and, on the eve of His crucifixion, he thanked God for the cup (Matthew 26:27; Mark 14:23). His apostles learned and emulated and preached his gratitude. Paul said that we should give thanks always for all things (Ephesians 5:20), and he understood the connections between gratitude and joy (1 Thessalonians 3:9).

Gratitude and appreciation are two of those rare and beautiful qualities (not quantities) of which we have more as we give away more. Our own supply of quantities (material, mammon) decreases as we give of our quantities to others; but our supply of each Christ-like quality (love, joy, testimony, gratitude) increases as we give of our supply to others.

Gratitude is warmth and light. Christ showed it to his Father, aroused it in others, left it with us all as an example, along with a thousand daily blessings to apply it to.

We are quickly conscious of the lack of gratitude in others (particularly when it is us they owe gratitude to), yet sometimes we seem completely unconscious of our lack of gratitude to God. Sadly, it is ourselves we rob—of the joy of gratitude.

MONTH 3
HIS STRENGTH

"He . . . fasted forty days and nights"

WEEK 9 PHYSICAL ENDURANCE AND POWER

When we think of strength, what comes to mind? Physical strength and stamina? Mental strength to pursue a goal at great odds? Spiritual strength—an ultimate, inner power to fall back on?

By any aspect, the true measure of strength is the life of Jesus Christ. His strength was total, complete, profound, and all-encompassing.

Consider first the Master's physical strength. Much of our traditional Christian art portrays Jesus as frail, small, and delicate—an effort, perhaps, to depict his sensitivity and tenderness. But the Savior was, physically, strong enough to fast for forty days to begin his earthly ministry. While such an event most certainly required spiritual strength, it also demanded physical stamina.

One poem, though it contains only the impressions of the poet and partakes of poetic license, perhaps catches the dimension of physical vigor in the Savior's life. (*Fere* is an archaic word meaning companion or comrade):

Ha' we lost the goodliest fere o'all,
For the priests and the gallows tree;
Aye lover he was of brawny men,
O' ships and the open sea.

I ha' seen him drive a hundred men
Wi' a bundle o' cords swing free
That they took the high and holy house
For their pawn and treasury.

Ye ha' seen me heal the lame and blind
And wake the dead, says he.
Ye shall see one thing to master all:
How a brave man dies on the tree.

I ha' seen him cow a thousand men
On the hills o' Galilee.
They whined as he walked out calm between
Wi' his eyes like the grey o' the sea.

30

A master of men was the goodly fere,
A mate of the wind and sea.
If they think they ha' slain our goodly fere
They are fools eternally.
> (Ezra Pound, "Ballad of the Goodly Fere,"
> portions only)

The Savior's physical strength certainly was impressive. Imagine the stamina required to be always in the Spirit. (Sidney Rigdon, after experiencing a vision for an hour or so, was, in the words of Philo Dibble, "limp and pale, apparently as limber as a rag.")

Knowing, as we do, the strength needed to overcome even a single sin, imagine the strength required to take on the agony of all men's sins.

WEEK 10 MENTAL AND EMOTIONAL DISCIPLINE

Whatever our Lord's physical strength may have been, the power and discipline of his *mind* was even more overwhelming, perhaps to a level that our own minds cannot really comprehend but can only glimpse. Think for a moment of some of the examples we know.

The unwavering, straight-ahead rejection of Satan's strongest suggestions: Try to imagine the discipline needed to turn from bread after forty days of fasting.

The lifetime avoidance of the misuse of any power: Try to imagine the discipline required to go from the Last Supper to Calvary with no sleep and no food, under constant petty abuse as well as physical torment, yet to never tap the power that could have instantly stopped the abuse. ("Who, when he was reviled, reviled not. . . ." 1 Peter 2:23.) In essence, all of Christ's recorded temptations were attempts to cause him to misuse his power. Thus the marvel of his character lies not only in what he *did*, but in what he *refrained* from doing. (Try to imagine having a billion dollars and never spending one cent on yourself.)

The emotional power by which he rejected discouragement despite incredible odds: Try to imagine a small province (half the size of New Hampshire), ruled by a wild-eyed half-Israelite who is supervised by the world's most powerful empire. Emerging out of a carpenter's shop in the province's most despised corner comes one proclaiming himself as the Redeemer of humanity and the founder of an everlasting kingdom.

Try to imagine the inner strength necessary under those circumstances to stay *always positive, always optimistic* despite ever-growing persecution. The Lord suffered rejection by his own town, by his friends. He endured inadequate and shallow understanding even on the part of those closest to him. He knew that his own life and the lives of many of his followers would end violently (Mark 8:31; Matthew 10:17-22). We would expect from a person in those circumstances gloom, discouragement, or at least occasional moodiness or cynicism. Try to imagine such a one who showed none of these, ever.

The mental discipline by which he prepared in advance for every opportunity and every crisis: If it is true that one hallmark of greatness is inner preparation and planning prior to outward acts, try to imagine the supreme example of the Lord in the thirty-year preparation preceding his three-year ministry, in the quiet mountainside moments or seaside serenity that preceded some of his greatest miracles and greatest speeches, in the Gethsemane that preceded his Calvary.

The inner strength that allowed him to live the most misunderstood and lonely of lives: If it is true that "to be great is to be misunderstood" and if "the altitude of a mountain is the measure of its solitude," then try to imagine the loneliness of the Lord and the discipline required to "descend beneath them all" (D&C 122:8; Ephesians 4:9-10).

The incredible patience he showed toward those with him: Try to imagine doing what he did in spite of the inadequacy of the human instruments he worked with—men who wanted vengeance (Luke 9:54), who were steeped in Jewish tradition (Mark 7:13), who bickered over their relative status in the kingdom (Matthew 20:20-21; Mark 10:35-41), who misunderstood even at the Last Supper (Luke 22:24).

In essence, our Lord's mind was simply stronger than all that surrounded him. He always acted; he never reacted. No doubt he usually had the guidance and help of the other two members of the Godhead, yet we know there were times when he was left with only his own inner strength to conquer the world.

This he did, and because he did, we are!

WEEK 11 COURAGE, FEARLESSNESS

Emerson said: "A hero is one who, taking both his reputation and his life in his hands, will, with perfect urbanity, dare the gibbet and the mob, by the absolute truth of his speech."

The world and its history are filled with courage, with men and women who gave their lives for a cause. All shine as stars, but only as *stars* compared to the Master's *sun*, for he did more. He preached openly the purest truth to a closed and tradition-bound people. At the Last Supper he had only twelve with him. He saw these twelve waver. Then, because it had to be so, even his Father's spirit left him completely alone.

Yet he walked unwaveringly toward the cross, refusing the compromise, or the equivocation, or even the simple silence that might have saved him.

The Lord's courage was not of the grandstand variety. He did not enjoy or promote conflict. But when people forced conflict, the Lord sided unequivocally with truth; and, often, truth flew in the teeth of Pharisee tradition. Plucking corn on the Sabbath (Matthew 12:1), unclean foods (Mark 7:14-19), and ceremonial fasting (Matthew 6:16-18) all provided opportunities for lessons by the Master.

He was like the *noon* (the Mosaic Law was the *dawn*). Pharisee eyes, accustomed to twilight, shut themselves against a stronger light. The Lord characterized many Jewish traditions as being against God (Matthew 15:6). He said that a humble publican was justified in God's sight more than a proud Pharisee who fasted twice a week (Luke 18:9-14). He taught that man's relationship with God depends not on ceremonial things but on spiritual things.

To the honest in heart, Christ fulfilled the Mosaic Law, but to those steeped in politics and tradition, Christ turned everything upside down. He boldly began his phrases with, "It has been said by them of old time . . . but *I* say unto you. . . ." Imagine the hate this aroused in the hearts of men so tradition-bound that their last scene in history's greatest drama involved yelling "Crucify him" from the perimeters of Pilate's court (from the perimeters because to step onto his court would make them "unclean").

The Master was such a total example of courage that after he was gone the quality of boldness in his disciples quickly reminded people of him—at least, that may be the meaning of Acts 4:13. His oft-repeated admonition sums up the quality in two words: "Fear not."

Perhaps it was the Lord's knowledge of all things that gave him perfect courage, for indeed it has been said that men fear only that which they don't understand. Was it his knowledge? Yes, but there was one thing more, and he told us exactly what that was: "Perfect *love* casteth out fear" (1 John 4:18).

WEEK 12 *RIGHTEOUS INDIGNATION*

Was the Savior ever angry? Yes and no. No, he did not lose control, did not let passion or emotion rule, did not retaliate against those who abused him. But yes, he got angry in the sense of righteous indignation, the kind of controlled but powerful anger and action that repulsed temptation (Matthew 4:8-11); that rebuked any lack of compassion (Luke 16:19-23); that rebuffed those who took from the poor and loved their own honor (Luke 20:45-47); and that reprimanded strongly the double standards (John 8:3-11), the hypocrisy (Matthew 23:23-28), and letter-of-the-law-above-compassion attitudes (Mark 3:1-5).

Perhaps the most remembered illustration of his indignation is the time when the Master drove the merchants from his Father's house (John 2:13-17). Yet here, as always, there is no hint of loss of control.

Christ's anger undoubtedly was awesome, powerful, but with a great and much-needed *purpose*. Possibly (as in the spirit of D&C 121:43) it was frequently followed by an overflow of love that separated the Lord's hate of the deed from his love of the person. Matthew 23 shows Christ giving some harsh denunciations, yet it ends with a beautiful statement of his love.

Destructive anger is anger that is connected to hate. Christ's anger was inseparably connected to perfect love. He simply loved people too much *not* to feel indignation toward the things that would destroy them. Indeed, the Lord, being perfect, could not have avoided this sort of anger, for it is *wrong* to be complacent in the presence of wrong, and he was bound sometimes to express himself forcefully.

The Master turned his other cheek to those who persecuted and reviled *him*, but he turned the full force of his indignation upon the evils that could hurt and destroy those he came to save.

In the dawn of time, our Lord and his Father (our Father) exercised righteous indignation by casting out the one-third who fought against your free will and mine, against our ultimate progress and joy. The Lord's indignation on this earth was a continuation of that same pure love for us and that same pure rejection of all that could lead us astray.

35

MONTH 4
HIS SENSITIVITY

"Into a mountain apart to pray"

WEEK 13 *POETIC SENSITIVITY*

Picture the Master sitting by the seaside as the sun sets; in a boat a little way out, speaking to the multitude on the shore; on the side of a mountain, alone in prayer; going out of the city's dust and clamor to the peaceful beauty of Bethany; winding his way through a golden cornfield; withdrawing to the wilderness to pray.

Now hear the imagery of his words:

"How often would I have gathered thy children together, even as a hen gathereth her chickens under her wings" (Matthew 23:37).

"Consider the lilies of the field, how they grow . . . even Solomon in all his glory was not arrayed like one of these." (Matthew 6:28-29).

"The wind bloweth where it listeth." (John 3:8).

"Her branch is yet tender, and putteth forth leaves." (Mark 13:28).

He spoke of putting "a new piece of cloth unto an old garment" and of "children of light" (Matthew 9:16; John 12:36).

All that the Lord did had a clarity, a beauty, a sensitivity, a harmony with nature and earth. All that he said had the poetic qualities of awareness and vividness.

How in tune the Lord was! How in touch, how in time!

I wondered for years why it was that his sensitivity and love for the earth went so far beyond that of any man. Then one day I heard the phrase, "We love what we have made." The Lord saw beauty in all things partly because he *put* beauty in all things.

He loved nature—the fresh, the good, the pure, the majestic. He went alone to the mountains, to the seashore, to the deserts to regenerate, to be recharged by the calm serenity of his earth and by the peace of its spirit.

Ponder how such retreats could precede great outpourings of the Holy Spirit. (From the desert he comes, preaching with new power. From the seaside he comes, curing and healing. From the mountains he comes, walking on water.)

It has been said that poets can speak with true beauty only about the things they love. The Master loved all, and loved *us* all, and therefore was the most sensitive and beautiful poet of all time.

WEEK 14 *"EXTRA-CENTEREDNESS"*

To most of us, life is a series of mirrors wherein every situation, every person, is perceived in terms of self-interest: "How will that affect *me?*" "What can he do for *me?*"

The Master's life was a series of windows. He was totally "extra-centered" or "other-centered" instead of being self-centered. He came to teach *us*, to help *us*, to cure *us*, to love *us*, to save *us*. And he lost himself in those tasks. It was Emerson who said, "See how the masses of men worry themselves into nameless graves, while here and there a great, unselfish soul forgets himself into immortality." Certainly the Savior is the ultimate, literal example.

Jesus Christ not only *died* for us, he *lived* for us. Wanting only to bring to pass the immortality and eternal life of man, he had not the slightest personal ambition. He was uninterested in praise or publicity; except for the reward of our eternal happiness, he didn't care about reward. Because of this, and because of who he was, the Savior saw *into* people—into their fears, their sins, their feelings, their potentials. He saw behind the impetuousness into the strength of a Peter. He saw past the hated occupation into the loyalty of Matthew. He saw through the sins and weaknesses of all mankind into their eternal potential and into their sonship with God and their brotherhood with himself.

Knowing that Christ was perfect implies knowing that he was totally free from the sin of selfishness, a sin that holds or has held (at least partially) every other resident this earth has ever had. Selfishness is the dimming, darkening blanket flung softly and silently across our minds by Satan. Its forces of dark win many battles against the *light* brigades of charity and love. But though those forces win many battles they will lose the ultimate war because (in eternal time) "charity never faileth"; and the "extra-centeredness," the love, the windows shown us by Christ, will someday (a thousand-year day) transform this earth to a paradise, cresting on Christ's charity and submerging Satan's selfishness.

Not only did our Lord love *all* mankind, he loved *each* of mankind. He spoke in different ways and with different analogies, depending on the nature and understanding of his listeners. He viewed and judged and taught each man according to that person's unique situation. He praised the man who doubled two talents to four, and held him equal with the man who turned five into ten. He was as aware of the momentary opportunities to teach individuals as he was of his chances to speak to masses.

Men walk about in the world, their minds filled with "island thoughts" of themselves, of their territory. By comparison, Christ's thoughts were more like the sea—they surrounded and included the needs of all men, touching each, caring for each.

Never were the Savior's "windows" so powerfully obvious as when, in the very midst of Gethsemane's agony, he recognized a teaching moment with a disciple and *gave* what was needed—a lesson about willing spirit and weak flesh (see Mark 14:37-38). How could a man, bent under the assumption of mankind's sins, still think at that moment of an individual's needs? How, indeed! How could any *man?*

The final-line message of the Master's extra-centeredness is the sure feeling that if there had been only *one* person to save on this earth, only *me* or only *you*, Jesus Christ would still have made his great sacrifice for me or for you.

WEEK 15 GENTLENESS, PATIENCE, FORGIVENESS

It was Tennyson who spoke of "gentleness, which, when it weds with manhood, makes the man." In our Lord this wedding was supreme, for despite his strength and power he possessed the greatest tenderness and compassion of anyone who has lived on earth.

In fact, the consistency of his unconditional, unequivocal tolerance for every individual equaled his unconditional, unequivocal intolerance for every wrong, every evil. (His total love for one meant total war with the other.) Thus, "Whom the Lord loveth he chasteneth" (Hebrews 12:5-6).

Ponder for a moment the boundless and total nature of the Master's attributes in this respect.

His patience:

—with his apostles, who consistently misunderstood and misapplied and vacillated,

—with publicans and sinners, and with all who needed help, regardless of how long they took to heed his advice.

His forgiveness:

—for his disciples, even to the point of finding an excuse for them when they fell asleep at his darkest hour (Matthew 26:36-41),

—for all people and all sinners who could come to him,

—for even those who hung him on the cross (Luke 23:34).

On the surface, one would think that a perfect being—who made no error himself, who could look on sin with *no* degree of allowance, would be a great discourager both by his seemingly unmatchable example and by his seemingly unreachable demands. Why, then, was Christ the greatest *encourager* in human history?

41

Because of his complete gentleness, patience, and forgiveness (all of which show us a complete sensitivity even to parts of our nature we do not know, and all of which show us an unconditional love), he can chasten us without hurting us, as he did with Peter (see Mark 8:31-33).

Tact, diplomacy, and soft, indirect approaches are things men use to be sure others do not feel offense or dislike. Christ needed none of these because his love was so genuine and total that rebuke became *part* of it—an acceptable part because his love could not be doubted.

Perhaps, like electricity, God's Spirit does not flow *into* something that it can't flow *out* of. The Master seemed constantly ready to receive his Father's ''currents'' of gentleness, patience, and love, because they flowed so easily and so naturally out of him and *into* the hearts and minds of all he met.

WEEK 16 DEPTH OF FEELING

You and I feel our deepest, most soul-rending concern and pray our deepest, most soul-pouring prayers when we are in moments of personal crisis (the loss of a loved one, the illness or injury of a family member, or any sort of deep, personal need).

It is family/friend crisis that brings depth of feeling. Christ so knew himself as our literal elder brother that *all* human crisis, physical or spiritual, was family/friend crisis to him. What you and I might feel for a very sick brother, suddenly taken seriously ill, Christ felt for *every* sick child, for *every* ordinary beggar, for *each* soul-sick Pharisee. What you and I could feel only for our own brother or our own child, he felt, one hundred times over, for all men—for *each* man.

True sensitivity comes not from learned techniques or from Dale Carnegie rules of human relations. It comes from true and genuine and deep feeling. Our Lord felt all things to their maximum depth.

Perhaps nowhere does the powerful current of his feeling flow more strongly than in the seventeenth chapters of John and of 3 Nephi, where he prays for his apostles, for the little children, for the multitude. Indeed, the depth of joy and feeling cannot be written, for Nephi said it could not even be conceived (3 Nephi 17:17).

When scriptural description is given of people who are on the verge of destruction because of their wickedness, the phrase that is sometimes used is "past feeling" (see 1 Nephi 17:45). As people become hardened and calloused by selfishness and sin, they begin to lose not only their virtue but their feelings. Our Lord, who was free from *all* sin and *all* selfishness, carried with him the deepest and most moving feelings.

MONTH 5
HIS LOYALTY

"Thy will be done"

WEEK 17 HUMILITY AND HONOR TO THE FATHER

Evidences of humility and honor, of glory and gratitude, *from* Jesus the Christ *to* God the Father can be found on virtually every page of the four Gospels. Christ's humility consisted (as ours should) not of fear or timidity, but of a profound understanding of his relationship to God.

Christ had a knowledge of God as his Father (which brought him confidence) and he had a knowledge of God as the designer, owner, and center of *all* (which brought him humility). In Christ, these two qualities (confidence and humility), which we often think of as opposites, were perfectly linked. In fact, they were fused into one metal of enduring hardness and strength.

In John 14:28-31 Christ explains that the source of his loyalty to the Father is his *love* for the Father. His love is perfect, and thus his loyalty is perfect.

Throughout his earthly ministry, the Lord reminded us of his profound understanding of his relationship to the Father. His phrases were "the Father's will," "the Father's power." When there was danger of someone not understanding this, the Savior stated it so strongly and dramatically that none could misunderstand: "I can of mine own self do nothing" (John 5:30); "Why callest thou me good? there is none good but one, that is, God" (Matthew 19:17); "the Son can do nothing of himself" (John 5:19).

He tied righteousness rightly and directly to seeking the Father's glory (John 7:18). In this dispensation the same emphasis remains. The Lord revealed that only two things offend God: failure to keep God's commandments and failure to confess God's hand in all things (D&C 59:21).

Jesus Christ's perfect example is the perfect teacher. Every word, every action, every moment of his life and his eternity gives gratitude and glory to his Father—our Father.

WEEK 18 DEVOTION AND DEDICATION

It has been said that the difference between great and mediocre men is a *cause*. A cause lights the way, propels the mind, and gives color and scope to the otherwise selfish flatness of life.

The Savior's cause, of course, defies comparison with that of any mere mortal, because his cause was *the* cause, *the Father's* cause of bringing to pass "the immortality and eternal life of man" (Moses 1:39). His devotion to this cause began in the pre-earth life and is total, complete, and *perfect*—and will be so for the rest of eternity.

Ponder the magnitude of that cause—*mankind's eternal life*. Try to realize that giving of life is woven around and through all that we know of Jesus Christ. He created this earth, and helped to create the physical bodies we now inhabit, thus giving us mortal life, and sharing with us all the joyous forms of life that occupy his earth. He ransomed his perfect life for our imperfect ones, thus giving us immortal life through a univeral resurrection. He gave us his gospel and he leads his church, thus giving us the path and the opportunity for eternal life. He gave us covenants and ordinances, thus setting the way whereby we can obtain not only eternal *life* but eternal *lives* (see D&C 132:24). Perhaps the Lord's cause of giving life reaches its apex as we are given not only our eternal life but the power ourselves to give life in the celestial kingdom's highest realm (see D&C 132:19-22).

Examples of the Savior's singular dedication to his Father's cause (and his own cause) are everywhere in the scriptures: At age twelve, he was already concerned with his cause (see Luke 2:49). He reiterated timelessly his personal subservience to his cause and to his Father (see John 4:34, 12:26, 13:16) and the question of not fulfilling his commitment to the cause never occurred to him (John 18:11).

47

It was and is because of his own total-minded loyalty and single-minded priority that he could (and can) ask the same of us: seek first the *kingdom*. Don't serve two masters. Be with me or you are *against* me (see Matthew 6:24, 6:33, 12:30). When the message didn't penetrate, he said it more dramatically: sell all you have *and* follow me. Disregard even your parents for my sake (see Matthew 19:21, Luke 14:26).

When Christ was praised or complimented, he either transferred that praise to his Father or he used it as a chance to teach *us* his devotion by promising that *we* could be blessed if we would keep God's word as he has (see Luke 11:27-28).

Our Lord asked us all to join his cause. He asked us with his words; he asked us with his love; he asked us with his life.

WEEK 19 *"THY WILL BE DONE"*

One of my favorite sacrament hymns that we don't sing often enough goes:

When in the wondrous realms above
Our Savior had been called upon,
To save our world of sin by love,
He said, "Thy will, O Lord, be done."

The King of kings left worlds of light,
Became the meek and lowly one;
In brightest day or darkest night
He said, "Thy will, O Lord, be done."

No crown of thorns, no cruel cross
Could make our great Redeemer shun.
He counted his own will but loss,
And said, "Thy will, O Lord, be done."

We take the bread and cup this day,
In memory of the Sinless One,

And pray for strenth, that we may say,
As he, "Thy will, O Lord, be done."

(Hymns, no. 199)

The first words that scripture ascribes to Jesus Christ are: "Father, thy will be done" (Moses 4:1-2). The first words recorded in his mortal lifetime are: "How is it that ye sought me? wist ye not that I must be about my Father's business?" (Luke 2:49). Among the last recorded words he uttered in Gethsemane were: "Nevertheless, not as I will, but as thou wilt" (Matthew 26:39). The last words of his mortal life were: "It is finished" (referring to his completion of the Father's will; John 19:30).

His first recorded statement after his resurrection was an admonition not to touch him until he had returned to the Father—whose will he had done (see John 20:17). The last words before his final ascension urged in effect that his disciples do the Father's will as he had (Matthew 28:19-20).

Since Christ's loyalty sprang from love, it is not surprising that the "apostle of love," John, mentioned most often Jesus' loyalty to the Father (see John 4:34, 5:19, 5:30, 7:16-18, 8:28-29, 10:29-30, 11:42, 12:26-28, 12:44-49, 13:16, 14:28-31, 15:8, 17:1, 18:11).

His challenge to us, as always, was to do as he had done: to "do the will of him that sent me" (John 4:34). And his promise, clarion clear, is the greatest promise of the greatest joy: "For whosoever shall do the will of God, the same is my brother" (Mark 3:35).

WEEK 20 ONENESS

In our terminology, *total loyalty* is about as far as devotion can go. If X is totally loyal to Y, then:

X always does and says what Y would want him to do and say;

X always gives Y the credit;

X always devotes himself to Y's cause.

Somehow (we try to reach it with our minds) Christ's devotion to God was and is *more* than loyalty—it is *oneness*.

Perhaps the concept of oneness is not so hard to grasp as it first seems. If a mortal lifetime of loyalty could cause a person to think and act, let's say, 90 percent similar to his Lord, then could not an eternity of loyalty bring about a 100 percent similarity? an absence of difference? a *oneness?*

Christ said, ''I and my Father are one'' (John 10:30). He said, ''If ye had known me, ye should have known my Father'' (John 14:7). The perfection of his life testifies to the perfection of that oneness.

He offered us maximum hope by telling us through his prayer to the Father on our behalf (see John 17:20-21) that *we* can join that oneness.

MONTH **6**
HIS LOVE

"Love . . . as I have loved you"

WEEK 21 *CHRIST IS LOVE*

One of my most treasured possessions is a letter of love and counsel written to me by my father when he was on his deathbed. A focal point of that letter reads:

> The greatest thought that Christ left on earth is love.
> It surpasses everything else. If a person practices love,
> then everything else takes care of itself.

I have already mentioned the snowy Christmas Eve when I asked my four-year-old daughter why Jesus came to earth. She answered: "To show us how to love each other and to show us how it will work when we die."

Beyond his atonement, what is "the measure of the stature of the fulness of Christ" (Ephesians 4:13)? Perhaps more than all else, as my four-year-old implied, it is Christ's perfect love.

Not until Christ came (and since then, only *because* of him) could mankind know the full meaning of love.

Before his life, in most societies, "love" meant friendship, loyalty, affection for one's own. The Savior gave depth to the surface, dimension to the flat. He added charity, empathy, magnanimity. He added the hard, self-sacrificing elements of love to the easy, self-serving aspects.

The coin of love, in many earlier philosophies, had revenge on its other side. People expressed love for friends and colleagues, hatred and vengeance for enemies. Cicero dated his letters from the "happy event" of his enemy's (Claudius's) death. Xenophon, a favorite disciple of Socrates and Plato, praised and eulogized his hero Cyrus the Younger by saying, "No man ever did more good to his friends and more harm to his enemies."

Jesus Christ revolutionized the western world's concept of love. Since Christ, forgiveness has been acknowledged as one of the greatest virtues. Tennyson represents King Arthur as near perfect because Arthur forgives Guinevere after she has deeply wronged him. Christ's instructions to "turn the

52

other cheek'' and ''love your enemy'' have counterparts in many behavioral codes. Even governments and constitutions take the posture of ''reform rather than revenge.''

The Lord taught the world about true, unconditional love. He *acted* rather than *reacted*. When he saw unkindness in other people, he took it as a sure sign that they needed love and help.

As with all else (and somehow even *more* than with all else), he *was* all that he taught. He *is* love.

WEEK 22 CHARITY

How remarkable and how worthy of thought is Paul's first epistle to the Corinthians, where he lists nearly every great virtue and puts *charity* at the top of the list. He says that charity ''never faileth.'' He says that one who has ''all knowledge and faith'' still has nothing without charity. He says that charity is greater than faith or hope (see 1 Corinthians 13:2, 8, 13).

In later revelation, Christ himself holds forth charity as an absolute requirement for his work (see D&C 12:8). He tells us to be ''clothed'' with it (see D&C 88:125), and he says we can do nothing without it (see D&C 18:19).

How could any word, any concept, be that complete, that total, that preeminently important, that absolute? Mormon gives us the answer when he says that charity is ''the pure love of Christ'' (Moroni 7:47). That definition explains all, fulfills all.

''The pure love of Christ''—is there here a double meaning?

1. To love as Christ loved: purely, completely.
2. To love Christ—purely, completely.

Is it a double meaning, or do both meanings say the same thing? Only by loving Christ purely can we love as purely as

53

Christ does. Only by loving as purely as Christ does can we purely love Christ.

Another possible meaning emerges: Wasn't his pure love the love of his Father? Thus could not charity, the "pure love of Christ," mean also "the pure love of the Father"? Again a double meaning becomes single as we remember the concept Christ taught: "If you love me, you love him that sent me."

Let us examine *how* Christ loved, so that we can strive:

—to love as purely as he;

—to love him purely;

—to love his Father (our Father) purely.

Indeed, Christ's love *was* perfect, and indeed it *never* failed—not even when those in his own hometown called him crazy, deceitful, devilish; not even when fellow townspeople tried to throw him off the cliff (see Luke 4:28-29); not even when he was spat upon while Barabbas was released; not even when one of his own betrayed him with a kiss; not even upon the cross.

Christ's love was pure because it was totally selfless ("I lay down my life for the sheep"; John 10:15). Christ's love was pure because it was universal (he loved the rich and the poor, the strong and the weak). Christ's love was pure because it was intelligent (he gave that which would help, withheld that which would hurt). Christ's love was pure because it was individual (he taught and lived and died for *each* man as well as for *all* men).

Now go back to the previous paragraph and change every "was" to "is," because Christ's pure love "never faileth," and he loves us each today as much as any were ever loved.

The key to understanding Christ's love is to realize his intimate concern for us as his younger brothers and sisters. Perhaps you or I would give our life for our own little sister. She is small and defenseless, and perhaps if her life were threatened, we would be willing to give ours instead. Christ sees *each* of us in that way. Indeed, as we suggested earlier, if *you* were earth's only sinner, if no one but you needed the atonement, Christ would still have died on the cross to pay for *your* sins.

WEEK 23 *COMPASSION, EMPATHY*

Just as we cannot think of Beethoven without thinking of music, we cannot think of Christ without thinking of love. One of the most beautiful elements of Christ's love was (and is) his compassion and empathy. He always sacrificed his own needs for the needs of others: he always fed the hungry crowds, he always stayed a little longer. The awesomeness of his true perfection lies more in the good he never failed to do than in the wrongs he never did.

One great quality possessed by my dear wife (and by many other women) is a particular, beautiful, natural, deep-felt compassion for anyone small, or weak, or sick, or poor—an instant empathy, a tear-to-the-eye *caring* that causes her to reach out, to hold, to help. We see everywhere in Christ this compassion, this empathy, this gentleness, this "unto the least of these" attitude that teaches more than words ever could.

Consider Christ's love for children—a love that held them, and blessed them, and that was "much displeased" when they were mistreated or deliberately kept from him (see Mark 10:13-16). So tender was his love for little children that it caused him to weep, and so powerful was the same love that it brought down from heaven "angels . . . in the midst of fire" (see 3 Nephi 17:21-24).

Consider the compassion and love he showed for widows (see Luke 4:25-26, 21:3), for beggars (see Luke 16:20), for the poor or oppressed (see Matthew 11:5; Luke 4:18). Indeed, it is not Christ's love for certain categories of people that is so overwhelming; it is his love for *all* categories of people.

Where lies complete compassion? Is it in the love of the poor, the frail, the fatherless? or is there an even deeper, even stronger compassion in loving the sinner, even when the person hurt by the sin is you?

Christ loved the *ignorant* sinner enough to forgive and forget and teach him a better way. And he loved the *willful* sinner enough to correct and chasten him with plain, straightforward words.

Christ's compassion is so boundless that if we will open ourselves fully to it, it will flow in so deeply that we will *run over* and drip our compassion into the lives of others.

WEEK 24 MAGNANIMITY AND FRIENDSHIP

Chinese poet-philospher Li Hung Chang said: "The only problem with Christ is that His teachings are too lofty to be practical."

Napoleon is quoted as saying:

I have inspired multitudes with such devotion that they would have died for me. But to do this it was necessary that I should be visibly present. Christ, unseen, asks for the human heart . . . and all who sincerely believe in Him experience that remarkable, supernatural love toward Him.

Chang was overwhelmed, Napoleon mystified, by Jesus Christ's love, by the fact that no one was excluded from it and by the fact that all who truly felt it returned it.

Christ created the quality of magnanimity when he added to the easy love (of friends and comrades) the difficult love (of enemies and opposites) (see Luke 6:27-38). His love overpowered hard-to-love people. His forgiveness was instant and total (see Matthew 18:21-22), and it flourished even on the cross (see Luke 23:34). His friendship extended even to his betrayer (see Matthew 26:50).

It is because of Christ's love for *all* that he can ask *all* to love him by loving each other. And indeed he did ask this: "Love your enemies" (Luke 6:27, 35); "Do good to them that hate you" (Matthew 5:44); and, perhaps most striking and challenging of all, "Love one another; as I have loved you" (John 13:34-35).

Did Christ's life leave any clues, any keys to the seemingly impossible door leading to the love of everyone and the hate or resentment of no one?

Yes. One key is found in the example Christ set of finding reasons for appreciating people. Christ spoke approvingly of loyalty (see Mark 10:29-30). He commended the use of talents (see Matthew 25:14-23). He saw good in things as small as the widow's mite (see Mark 12:43), and in things as large as the hidden power and quality of his apostle Peter.

Another key is the way Jesus could believe in people even when they did not believe in themselves (see Luke 5:8-10).

Still another key ties into the practice of praying earnestly for other people: for friends (see Luke 22:32; John 17:9), and also for the unworthy (see Matthew 5:44).

A final key (and perhaps the greatest) comes to us as we learn to view all men as friends and as brothers (see Matthew 5:21-24).

What a blessing (and an incentive) it is to know that, as we make friends with the least of our brothers, we are making friends with the greatest (and most senior) of our brothers (see Matthew 25:40).

MONTH 7
HIS LEADERSHIP

"Come . . . follow me"

WEEK 25 CHARISMA

Close your physical eyes for a moment and let your mind's eye visualize the Savior:

1. Speaking to groups of people with such spell-binding power that the officers sent to arrest him simply become part of the enthralled audience. (Later, in trying to explain to the Pharisees why they did not take him, the officers are able only to say "Never man spake like this man"; John 7:46).

2. Teaching principles with such inner force that his enemies nervously report, "He stirreth up the people" (Luke 23:5), and that his disciples feel in their hearts such singular devotion that one cries to the others, "Let us also go, that we may die with him" (John 11:16).

3. Riding into Jerusalem with the inexpressible dignity and power that draws multitudes "saying, Hosanna," and that creates a scene such that "all the city was moved" (Matthew 21:6-10).

Dictionaries define *charisma* as "a personal magic of leadership arousing special popular loyalty or enthusiasm for a public figure; a special magnetic charm or appeal" (*Webster's New Collegiate Dictionary*).

From whence did Christ draw his supreme charisma? Was it from his actual spoken words? from his physical stature and presence? from the white-heat brilliance of his insight and teaching? Yes, it was all of these perhaps, but it was from at least two more things:

1. A love so unconditional and so universal, yet so individual, that all who contacted it *felt* it.

2. A basic realness—an open, straightforward candor and honesty-with-self that removed any hesitation and that attracted people like a magnet.

WEEK 26 GOALS AND PLANS

For many years, I have worked in management planning, producing written documents that define and clarify an organization's goals and that lay out a detailed plan for how to achieve those goals. I judge a plan by its completeness, its consistency, its clarity, it creativity, and its comprehension of all factors and elements. I operate on the theory that those for whom I write a plan will be stronger leaders because of the efficiency and confidence which comes from having a clear course to follow.

Thus I am an admirer of plans.

The plan championed before this world by the Savior was and is perfect. It is at once both incomparably complete and incomparably simple. It provides a wondrous physical sphere complete with the elements and the agency necessary in the proving/learning process that progresses us toward our Father. Its patriarchal order establishes a linked eternal organization with each man "trunked" between his roots and his branches. Its laws shape discipline and character, and its fall and its ransom build dependency-magnified love.

Perhaps part of the power and perfection of Christ's leadership comes from the power and perfection of the plan, the plan of the Father which, through total commitment to it, Christ had in effect made his own. Part of the reason that he never faltered is that the plan has no faults. Nothing has been overlooked, no thing and no *one* has been left out.

We know through Abraham that the Lord reaches all goals that he sets (see Abraham 3:17), and we know through Paul that *we* can reach our righteous objectives if we have the Lord's help (see Philippians 4:13).

It would seem that Christ, as Jehovah, planned the things which he did, creating each element spiritually before it was created physically upon the earth (see Moses 3:5).

61

In trying to comprehend this facet of the Lord, we must not only think of his perfection in the use of goals and plans, we must also strive to grasp the magnitude of his cause—the totality of his commitment.

To try to compare Christ's cause or plan to the cause and plan of any man is like comparing the earth to a grain of sand.

Daniel H. Burnham said:

Make no small plans . . . they have no magic to stir men's blood and probably themselves will never be realized. Make big plans . . . aim high and hope and work. Remember that a noble, logical diagram, once recorded, will never die, but long after we are gone it will be a living thing, asserting itself with ever growing consistency.

Christ's power of leadership and his charisma come partly from his incomparable cause, the all-encompassing plan: "to bring to pass the immortality and eternal life of man" (Moses 1:39).

WEEK 27 TOTAL EXAMPLE

Someone once defined leadership with perfect simplicity: "Leadership is being." The related clichés are endless: "Practice what you preach," "Ask no one to do something you would not do," "What you are speaks so loudly I cannot hear what you say," "You can't lead someone to a place you are not going."

There has never been any other teacher who could, as the Savior did, summarize all he had taught in three words: "Come, follow me" (Matthew 4:19; Luke 18:22). All other leaders, at times, either directly or by implication, have had to say, "Do as I say, not as I do."

Perhaps this thought prompted Napoleon, who is quoted as saying:

I know men, and I tell you that Jesus Christ is not a

man. . . . A resemblance does not exist. There is between Christianity and [all other] religions a distance of infinity. Everything in Christ astonishes me. His spirit overawes me and His will confounds me. Between Him and [anyone] else in the world there is no possible term of comparison.

It is infinitely easier to set a perfect example in negatively phrased physical teachings (what not to do physically—"don't kill," "don't steal," and so on) than to exemplify positively phrased mental teachings (what *to* do, in mind as well as in action—e.g., "love your fellow man"). In the second category, perfection is ruined by one moment's unkind thought, or by one single failure to notice a need and fill it, or by one single failure to recognize a chance to do good and do it.

Jesus Christ lived a *perfect life:* a fact that is remarkable because he never committed sin, but much more remarkable because he never *omitted* good.

The one thing that makes the challenge "Be ye therefore perfect" credible is the simple fact that he who *said* it, *did* it.

WEEK 28 *REVOLUTIONARY UNIQUENESS*

Prior to Christ's ministry, people were told to love their friends; Christ taught them to love not only their friends, but their enemies. People were admonished not to kill; Christ taught them not to feel anger. They were commanded not to commit adultery; Christ taught them not to lust. Under the Mosaic Law of revenge, the code permitted "an eye for an eye"; Christ taught a superior code of turning the other cheek.

Christ replaced ten "shalt nots" with one all-encompassing "shalt": love.

When Jesus brought his gospel to the earth, it was not ten degrees different—it was (often) opposite. In fact, it was more than just a change in *degree;* it was a change in *kind.* It was radical and it was revolutionary (in the highest and purest and most extreme use of the terms). It carried no compromise, no adjustment for tradition, no tactful attempt to find "common ground" or "previous precedent." Indeed, it would be hard to coin a more directly revolutionary preface than the one Christ so often used; "Ye have heard that it was said by them of old time, . . . but I say unto you . . ." (Matthew 5:21-22).

It was not only the content of his teachings that was unique. It was:

His orientation—always to the positive, to "what *to* do," never to the negative. He was concerned with *omission* as much as, or more than, with *commission.*

His motivation—the love and joy in serving God, not the fear and restriction used by other religionists to hold their flocks.

His style—he was not a pacifist without action, not a reactionary without thought, rather the perfect blend of thought *and* action: saying *and* doing, condemning *and* changing.

His consistency—he was not a product of the general attitude or tone of the times, as most revolutionaries are. Changes around him had no effect on his cause or his teachings. He always *acted*, never *reacted.*

His method—he did not use power or political influence and force or any other common revolutionary method. He did not try to start with kings or rulers. He was content to leave the full weight of his message in the hearts of a few simple men, knowing that its light and effervescence would bubble up through any and all obstacles until it lighted and engulfed the earth.

Renan, certainly with some of these elements in mind, said: "Jesus is in every respect unique . . . and nothing can be compared with Him. To tear His name from this world would be to shake it from its very foundations."

MONTH 8
HIS TEACHING

"He taught them as one having authority"

WEEK 29 PREPARATION

It was Lindberg who said "Preparation precedes power," but it could have been said by anyone—anyone great enough to make real contributions.

Again, as with everything else, Christ epitomized and perfected this quality. He underwent thirty years of preparation before his ministry began—and that preparation was mental, emotional, social, and physical as well as spiritual. And as his ministry began the pattern of preparation continued—in mountain-top solitude, at seaside, in desert, or simply within the peace of his own mind. Frequently we observe a calm, inward, strength-gathering moment preceding miracles, sermons, temptations.

The Lord's preparation started long before this world was made. We know little of what it entailed, but we *do* know that, here on earth, his preparation was total and constant. His mental preparation was so extensive that he could out-quote his Pharisee adversaries from what they considered to be their own books. He *knew* the law that he came to fulfill, and he knew people, so that he always began where they were—on *their* level, talking first of things they understood and accepted, using analogies, parables, and metaphors with which they could quickly relate. All of this he was able to do because of his preparation.

Part of the explanation of Christ's unwavering, sharply focused power was his total preparation. Most men have known those beautiful, sure moments when tight preparation brought tight confidence. Christ's perfect confidence stemmed from his perfect preparation.

WEEK 30 *UNDERSTANDING*

A good teacher understands—he understands his topics or subject matter, his listeners, their needs, and his relationship with them.

A great teacher not only understands but enlarges the understanding of those he teaches.

Today, extensive academic fields of "behavioral science" have grown up around "human relations." A great branch of the medical field concerns itself with psychology and psychiatry. Books by the thousands are printed and distributed on how to relate, how to listen, how to motivate, how to empathize, how to communicate, how to compliment, how to encourage, how to make friends. Yet all the books and branches and academic fields are somehow encompassed and surpassed by Christ's simple examples and teachings on *how to love*.

Christ's tolerance and understanding enabled him to see offensive characteristics as sure signs that someone needed help.

He thought of and taught each person as an individual. He listened with his eyes and his heart as well as with his ears. And thus, using his divine powers, he knew people instantly—not only their characters but the background of their lives (see John 4:17-19).

Through this tremendous understanding, Jesus taught specific people according to their specific needs: He told the rich young ruler that he should sell all that he had and give it to the poor and follow him (see Luke 18:18-22). He told a sinner who felt the possibilities of repentance to go and sin no more (see John 8:11). He told Peter through unforgettable question-and-answer repetition to take over leadership and feed His sheep (see John 21:15-17).

Because he understood individual souls, he taught specific, personal needs in the particular way that each individual could understand. Because he understood, he *was* un-

67

derstood, and thus we now understand him as the greatest teacher the world will ever know.

WEEK 31 IMAGERY, VITALITY, POWER

Never man spake like this man" (John 7:46) reported the Jewish officers to the Pharisees. Indeed, never before or since has a man spoken or taught as the Lord did. His audiences, whether a silent multitude or a single man, were *held*, alert and spellbound, by the power of his parables, the penetration of his points.

He took the common things that all his listener's hands and eyes had touched (the leavened bread, the lilies of the field, the vineyard workers, the mustard seed) and wove them into brilliant shafts of light that pierced the hearts of blind-minded men.

It is clearly a miracle that Christ, knowing all, could communicate perfectly with those knowing relatively little, and it is even more of a miracle that he could communicate equally and simultaneously to both the simple and the learned even when he found them side by side in the same audience.

His parables, perfectly crafted, conveyed knowledge to the listener in exact proportion to the listener's faith and intelligence; thus those around him were always warmed and filled to *their* capacity (whatever their capacity). For a period, Christ spoke only in parables (see Mark 4:34), a technique which served as a filter and which sifted out the true *hearers* who became the disciple-extensions of his word.

Along with its singular sensitivity and intricate imagery, Christ's teaching carried explosive power. His hearers were lifted, carried away, even moved to the point of willingness to die for him (see John 11:16). When he was ready to cease, Christ's compassion moved him to keep speaking, to keep helping, and then the response and reaction of the people recharged him so that his power and work and spirit continued drawing the people higher and closer to himself (see 3 Nephi 17).

It would appear that the Savior had a powerful, resonant voice. Anyone who has tried to talk above the constant sound of any lake or body of water would know the power required of a voice to speak from a floating boat to a multitude on the shore (see Matthew 13:1-3). Yet Christ's voice is often described as soft—perhaps soft like the low volume of a high-voltage amplifier—with such power behind the softness that it penetrated the heart and seemed to come from inside rather than outside the listener's mind.

We must simply try to *feel* the power of his teaching, because even those who were eyewitnesses could not describe it: "The eye hath never seen, neither the ear heard, before, so great and marvelous things . . .

"And no tongue can speak, neither can there be written by any man, neither can the hearts of men conceive so great and marvelous things . . . and no one can conceive of the joy that filled our souls" (3 Nephi 17:16-17).

WEEK 32 *TRUTH AND LOVE*

Would not the truest, surest definition of *teacher* be "one who plants *truth* in other minds and hearts"? Within that definition is a harder word to define. What is "truth"? For centuries philosophers have sought a workable, complete meaning. The author of truth—sometimes himself called "the Word"—defined it: "Truth is knowledge of things as they are, and as they were, and as they are to come" (D&C 93:24).

It is truth that glorifies man (see D&C 93:28) and truth that makes us free (see John 8:32). Intelligence is the combination of light and truth: light comes from truth, and truth from light, and the two together (truth and light) are the glory of God (see D&C 93:29, 36).

Light *is* truth, and truth is light. The light of Christ permeates the whole earth and at least *touches* the heart of every man, both as a conscience and as a discerner of truth. Things that are right have a clarity, a feeling of rightness, a ring of truth like the clarion sound of a bell on a clear morning. Truth not only rings like a bell, it *rings* like a circle—its ends connect. It is consistent with other truth. All truth is "one eternal round" (D&C 35:1; 1 Nephi 10:19).

The thing that sets Christ apart from all other teachers of all other times (even more so than his preparation and his imagery and his power) was the profound ring of truth in all that he said. It stopped men in their tracks; it pried open tightly closed minds; it was a sweet, clear note in a world of confused disharmony. Christ the teacher never found it necessary to defend or debate his points. Each one carried itself by its own ring of truth; each one vibrated with the tonal frequency that could penetrate the material of mind and heart and soul.

There is one final quality that completes the picture and that further sets Christ apart as an incomparable teacher: Behind the ring and power of his words was total love for those he taught. Just to hear the force and thrust of perfect truth was one thing; but to feel behind it the warmth of deep, personal love was something more, and it was this warmth that made the Lord's teaching irresistible to the sincere (and threatening to the hypocritical).

Ponder this aspect of the Savior's life by imagining him on the Mount. Each short phrase resounded in the ears of the listeners with pure truth; many eyes were transfixed on the light of his face; those hearts, for the moment at least, were lifted above, away from the lower earth, carried on the wings of his love.

MONTH 9
HIS LIGHT

"Ye are all the children of light"

WEEK 33 *INTELLIGENCE*

In the pre-earth life there was one spirit, the firstborn spirit of the Father, who was ''more intelligent than they all'' (Abraham 3:19). Elder B. H. Roberts felt that this scriptural passage means that Christ was (and is) more intelligent than *all* the others—more intelligent than the combined intelligence of all the rest.

This one great Being understood the nature of us, his brothers and sisters, so well, and he understood the mind and will of his Father so well, that he was able to be the premortal advocate of the Father's great plan of agency, choice, and atonement.

Further, his intelligence was (and is) supreme, so that he was (and is) able to *implement* that plan.

Still further, his intelligence is complete, so that it literally lights the world, penetrating with its brightness the depths of earth and opening men's minds to scientific discovery, to artistic sense, to spiritual truth.

Even the world's secular history demonstrates the light of Christ and reveals the particular periods when his light was accepted by man in its greatest abundance. Because of the seeking nature of men, the door of the Dark Ages was opened a crack, and rays of light poured forth and sparked the mind-opening periods of Renaissance and Reformation. Then, as the full gospel was restored, the door was flung wide, and we entered a period that represents only 3 percent of mankind's history yet contains perhaps 97 percent of his inventions and discoveries.

Christ's intelligence lights the world. It was and is the source of man's clearest insights. It was gained by our Savior through an eternity of excellence, and he now uses that intelligence to bring to pass the immortality and eternal life of you and me.

WEEK 34 *LIGHT OF TRUTH*

Perhaps this facet of Christ's character transmits the same light as the facet previously discussed, for *intelligence* has been defined by the Lord as "the light of truth" (D&C 93:29).

The Savior referred to himself in three ways:

1. "The Son of man" or "the Son of God" (meaning the Son of exalted man, the literal offspring of God the Father in the flesh);
2. "Life" (for he gives life to all); and
3. "Light" (for light also he gives to all).

When Christ says that he is Light and when we speak of the "light of Christ" or the "light of truth" or the "light of the gospel," there is much more than *symbolic* truth contained in those descriptions. Christ is more than a symbol of light or an analogy with light: he is the *source* of light (and *light* is far more than what we know it to be).

He is responsible for the light our eyes see, and he is responsible also for the light our minds see. These two types of light are related: they both illuminate and they both come from the same source. All that awakens, opens, cleans, energizes, brightens, frees, and lifts is light. All that illuminates and brings joy is light—just as all that closes, confines, dims, hides, or hurts is darkness.

Christ's influence is an army of light—a light brigade that aims to shine into every corner and every mind.

One cannot think about or ponder the true Christ without feeling both the brightness and the warmth of the light. I feel it as I write and you feel it as you read; but even more, each of us feels it when we pray.

Not only can things we see be classified as light or dark: things we hear and things we feel can also be thus classified. Gospel principles, moral thinking, even mathematical or

73

logical facts have a "ring of truth"—a *light* of truth about them that is unmistakable to one in tune with the Spirit.

There is not a phrase of scripture from our Lord that does not carry that light, that ring of truth; and there was not an action or thought in his life that did not reflect and magnify its brightness.

WEEK 35 CLARITY AND COMPREHENSION

We have thought and spoken already of the brilliant focus and imagery of Christ's teaching and speaking, but the intelligence of his words went far beyond. What he said seemed brighter than the world and larger than life. One senses a depth of clarity in his words—a depth of clarity that is like looking down through a hundred feet of sunlit water and seeing everything in sharp, and somehow magnified, detail.

His eyes were clear—

his thoughts were clear—

his purpose was clear.

And each of the three comprehended everything.

We, each of us in his own way, tend to *fear* whatever we don't understand. It is said, too, that we love whatever or whomever we *do* come to understand. If we accept these two statements, it follows that one who comprehended all would fear nothing and would love everything.

Did Christ's total comprehension precipitate his total love? or was it vice versa? Did both develop together, or did they develop separately? Whichever it was, Christ's comprehension and love brought about in him a clarity that set him apart from the children of men. "Never man spake like this man" (John 7:46).

The Savior was a master of reason, of logic, of the simple and direct word.

As we learn to think *clearly* of his *clarity*, our own minds will clear and we will give our hearts and our lives to him.

WEEK 36 GLORY

The glory of God is intelligence . . ." (D&C 93:36). What a remarkable statement—remarkable when we come to realize that God is different from man not in *kind*, but in *degree*. He is not of a different species, but rather he is the epitome, the maximum of the *same* species.

God's glory, Christ's glory, which sets them so far above us, springs not from their differences from us but from their *similarities* with us, from their successful completion of the very experiences we are now undergoing.

All great prophets—from ancient times to modern times, from east to west—have tried (as far as mere words will allow) to describe, or at least to declare, the *glory* of God. In other words, any who have glimpsed the majesty of God or Christ or of their kingdoms become so overwhelmed that, from then on, they praise and voice the Lord's glory.

Those of us who are just beginning to know the Savior can begin to feel his glory as we read his words. As we do we should try to realize that even as celestial glory now surrounds him on his heavenly throne, so also did a certain glory surround him in his carpentry shop, and on Peter's boat, and on the dusty road to Jerusalem. His glory lies in what he knows, in his comprehension of the elements and the spirit, and in his oneness with the Father.

More than that, his glory lies in the great and eternal cause that he shares with the Father—the cause of bringing to pass "the immortality and eternal life of man" (Moses 1:39).

MONTH 10
HIS PRIORITIES

"My kingdom is not of this world"

WEEK 37 ETERNAL FRAME OF REFERENCE

A child, living and seeing in the moment, wants the candy *now*. A parent, with slightly wider vision, sees no appetite for dinner and another cavity in the teeth.

We children, during our turn on earth, see (and want) the material, physical world. Our Father and our Elder Brother see eternal purpose and the things we must gain to return to them.

Therefore, Christ says to us, "lay up for yourselves treasures in heaven, where neither moth nor rust doth corrupt" (Matthew 6:20). What an example was his life—free from the things that the world calls great, but filled with the light and life that lasts long after earth's glories fade!

Christ saw all things in their true perspective, in the eternal frame of reference. Thus those who broke laws, who went wrong, who hurt him, who crucified him were not enemies to be fought but friends who needed help—brothers and sisters whom he had come to save.

It was as though Christ, even with his feet on the earth, preserved his vision from above so that he saw more than the moment and based his feelings and his actions on eternal rather than on mere earthly realities.

The enemies, in his frame of reference, were never the *people* he had come to save. Instead, the enemies were always the *evils* that could hurt those people and that could block the salvation he sought for them. Hypocrisy, greed, sin—these were the destroyers, the things Christ came to subdue.

Try for a moment to glimpse things from his perspective—a perspective of being fully aware of the realities of the premortal life, the spirit world, the degrees of glory:

   —evil becomes a need for help
   —enemies become brothers and sisters who misunderstand

—death becomes birth
—leadership becomes service
—God becomes Father
—children become respected brothers and sisters
—pain and opposition become purpose and joy
—families become eternal organizations
—weakness becomes humility and potential spiritual strength
—earthly riches become mind-diverting things with no value unless they are used to help and serve
—wisdom, understanding, and intelligence become part of the eternal soul—things that last
—faith, hope, and charity become passports back to the Father.

One reason that Christ's life was so different from any man's is that he saw the whole circle of eternal life—360 degrees—while we so often see only the narrow slice of the moment.

WEEK **38** FAMILIES

It is interesting and instructive to note that God, from all the titles or names available to him, chose to have us call him *Father*.

During our Savior's ministry he spoke of eternal relationships in *family* terminology, and through the restored gospel we have received further enlightenment on these concepts: God is our *father;* Christ is our eldest *brother;* and we are, to each other and to Christ, *brothers* and *sisters*.

In Christ's church, the family is the center, the focal point, the foundation. Church meetings, programs, manuals, and teachings cluster and concentrate around the family.

Why, then, is there not more evidence in Christ's life of a family orientation, and why did he say: "He that loveth father or mother more than me is not worthy of me'' (Matthew 10:37); ''no man that hath left house, or brethren, or sisters, or father, or mother, or wife, or children . . . for my sake, and the gospel's, but he shall receive an hundredfold'' (Mark 10:29-30); ''The father shall be divided against the son, and the son against the father; the mother against the daughter'' (Luke 12:53)?

Answer: There *is* evidence of family orientation in the Savior's life—widespread, abundant evidence. And he contrasted the gospel with the family because the family was the most important, the greatest value comparison he could use.

The Lord's concern for families is frequently manifest in the scriptures. When Jesus, as Jehovah, gave the Ten Commandments and when he reiterated them again during his earthly ministry, several of them had connotations for the stability of the family, and one carried with it the promise, ''Honor thy father and thy mother: that thy days may be long'' (Exodus 20:12).

Scriptures that some take as a ''put-down'' of families (see Mark 10:29, Luke 12:53) are actually Christ's most stirring family tributes. He is undoubtedly grieved that the gospel would break up some families; he shows approval for those who have to leave their families to follow him; and his most dramatic way of showing the importance of following him is to compare it with the *next* most important thing in life: the family!

Coming to Christ, knowing him, following his teachings, is life's highest priority—it is the *only* priority higher than family. As D&C 93:44 and other scriptures would suggest, the family should take priority over church programs and organizations; and this priority, properly viewed and carried out, is a part of keeping the commandments of Christ.

Why did Christ not make even more effort to spell out these priorities? Perhaps because they dovetail so tightly with everything else he taught that there was no need. His gospel *is* the family; the family *is* his gospel. They are not com-

80

petitors but *teammates*, and the Savior is both captain and coach, support and star.

He said, "Seek ye first the kingdom of God" (Matthew 6:33). How better can we do that than by helping God's other children (especially our own children) to return to him?

WEEK 39 RELATIONSHIPS ABOVE ACHIEVEMENTS

The Savior knew well that *relationships* are eternal. He also knew that worldly achievements are temporary and, in themselves, superfluous, and that they often lead men to forget who they are in *relationship* to God.

As builder, associate designer, and owner of the world (and more importantly as our Elder Brother) Christ gave us the greatest eternal advice of all time: "Seek the things of the kingdom of heaven." The kingdom of heaven consists of *relationships*—with God, with self, with family, with others.

He said it with words, but to really say it he lived it. In the entire scriptural record of his life there is no hint that he ever sought an "achievement" of the world (a *thing*), and there is no hint that he ever overlooked or passed by a relationship (a *person*).

If "achievements" are described as "things done for self," Christ had none. The only achievements that he ever made were of the variety that helped others, that gave true joy.

He "achieved" the greatest speech ever given (Matthew 5).

He "achieved" the perfect, exemplary life.

He "achieved" the Atonement.

One of the most remarkable aspects of the Savior's perfect earthly life was the constant correctness of his every decision—not only major decisions, not only basic right/wrong decisions, but the infinite number of small, multialternative little decisions. He always knew the *best* thing to say

81

to *this* person at *this* minute. He always knew the most constructive way to spend the next five minutes.

One of the little decisions everyone has to make every day is the choice between a relationship and an achievement. (Should I talk to the friendly person next to me on the bus, or should I read my paper? Should I stop to help the little boy, or should I finish my project and let his mother take care of him?)

Christ always chose the relationship, the *person*. When he was going somewhere and someone asked for some time, he stopped. When he met a stranger, regardless of how busy he was, he got to know that person.

He lost himself, lost his personal desires, lost his achievements, lost his *life* for us, for his relationship with us, for our eternal relationship with him and with our Father.

WEEK 40 *"SEEK YE FIRST"*

The core of what Christ taught and what he lived is this admonition: "But seek ye first the kingdom of God, and his righteousness" (Matthew 6:33). As he spoke on the Mount, he turned the world upside down, elevating the low, leveling the high, calling for treasure in the heart (see Matthew 6:21), and telling those who thought they owned the world that they owned nothing. The true in heart felt the light and knew that moth and rust and time would take all their *quantities* and leave them, in the eternities, with only their *qualities*: qualities gained through the seeking, *first*, of the kingdom of God.

Christ couldn't have *really* taught that principle if he had not lived it. But he *did* live it—so totally that *we* know *he* knew whereof he spoke. He sought nothing of the world: no mammon, no honors or recognitions or titles, no praise, no physical possession, no power, no comfort or ease.

He consistently, consciously, continuously sought the kingdom of God and its righteousness not only for himself but for all his younger brothers and sisters. His goal—our eternal life and exaltation—was reflected in all he said, and, more remarkably, in all he did.

Throughout the ages, saints and sages have proposed *discipline* as the key to the highest realm of life: "Deny yourself." Deny your own needs for the sake of someone who needs you. Deny the momentary pleasure for the sake of the longer term. Deny the easy and mediocre for the difficult and excellent. Deny the physical for the spiritual. Christ's life is the maximum study of self-denial—not self-harm or self-apathy, but the denial of personal gratification, the denial of his life for ours.

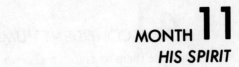

WEEK 41 CONFIDENT HUMILITY

We often use them as antonyms: *confident* as one extreme, one pole, *humility* as the other. In our Lord they combined, merged, fused, and became (in a way) synonyms.

How could these opposites, each practiced to perfection, coexist in one being? Simply because they are not opposites. Christ proved that.

Let us first consider the Savior's confidence. It is hard to imagine a more total assurance or sureness than that of a being who indicates he is the only one who really knows God; accepts the title of ''Messiah'' (Mark 8:29); states in so many words that he will come in glory with angels (Matthew 25:31); prophesies that those who are ashamed of him, he will be ashamed of (Luke 9:26); and affirms that his word will never pass away (Mark 13:31).

The Savior's confidence is what generated his charisma. He never doubted himself or his cause. People around him felt it, were lifted by it, gravitated toward it. Indeed the greatest measure of Christ's complete self-security and confidence is his perfect ability to spend all of his thought and time serving and helping and changing others, to spend none of it worrying about himself.

On the other hand, consider his humility. He said he was ''meek and lowly'' (Matthew 11:29). He admonished *us* to be meek (see Matthew 5:15) and humble as a child (see Matthew 18:4). Paul spoke of ''the meekness and gentleness of Christ'' (2 Corinthians 10:1).

Yet that same Paul wrote that the Lord gave not the spirit of fear, ''but of power, and of love, and of a sound mind'' (2 Timothy 1:7).

To understand, we need to stop thinking of humility and confidence as opposites. We need to consider the fact that both, in their most complete and perfect form, spring from the same source—and that source is a true understanding of one's relationship to the Father.

To know God the Father, and to understand our relationship to him, brings two inevitable results: the confidence of being literal offspring of God, and the humility of comparing his perfected level with our "beginner's level." Perfect love of God (which is the same as knowing him) brings confidence because it *"casteth out fear"* (1 John 4:18). Perfect love of God also causes humility because it brings us to "all lowliness and meekness" (Ephesians 4:2). Christ, who not only knew and loved the Father but who was "with him" (John 8:16) and who was one with him (John 10:30, 17:21), thus reached maximum levels both in confidence and in humility.

WEEK 42 PEACE

Picture the Savior at the seaside of Galilee, sitting alone, his finger tracing the sand, his ear aware of the small lapping waves, his eye reflecting the peace around him (and in him).

Key words in the promises he made to men were *rest, easy, light,* and *peace.* His most common greeting (or farewell) was "peace be with you" (John 14:27).

In our own dispensation, one of his greatest promises is that those who serve him will know "the peaceable things . . . which bringeth joy, that which bringeth life eternal" (D&C 42:61).

The feeling of the Holy Ghost is often best described as peaceful—a soft, sure, warm knowing. Indeed that Spirit—in our prayers, in church, during the sacrament—may be our most powerful witness of *Christ's* Spirit and the deepest insight into his personality of wonderful calmness and peace.

In physical things as well as in personality things, there is an interesting connection between *peace* and *depth.* The lower reaches of a great sea are always calm, even while a tempest rages on its surface. One source of the Lord's abiding peace was the tremendous depth of his character. When Christ taught something, the thought was so complete, so perfectly formed, that it was like a bubble that began deep in the still depths of his soul and then rose through the calm, gaining clarity and sparkle as it ascended until it burst brightly to the surface with power and perfect beauty.

Most of us, at one time or another, have met a person so at peace with himself that he calmed *us:* one whose spirit quieted our spirit. Anyone who has felt that has liked it, and has wished for it again. As we draw close to Christ, as we come to know him, we will understand the source of his peace, and his peace will be ours.

WEEK 43 CALMNESS

As much as the world's art misses in trying to depict Jesus, one thing it often catches is his supreme and sublime calmness.

As I write I'm looking at a print of a famous painting, and I think *calmness* is the first thing it portrays. Poetry, too, often feels this element, as in Ezra Pound's line describing Christ's departure, untouched from those who came to take him, "as He walked out calm between, wi' His eyes like the grey o' the sea."

The Lord was surrounded by an aura of calm. He calmed and softened and quieted all those with receptive hearts who came close to him. At will he calmed even the elements, the storm and the sea (see Luke 8:24). His *words* still calm us today, and his Spirit calms us even more so. The sweet peace of his life and his being somehow flows through prayer, through good works, and even off of the printed scriptural page and into our hearts. Often the *first* thing we truly know about Christ is the calmness of his peaceful Spirit.

He was like the *eye* of a hurricane. The things he taught (and their friction against the world) could strike with the force of wind and thunder all around, yet Christ, at the center, would move in total calm. He was always *acting*, never *reacting*—never letting the clamor or clatter or bow-string tension of the world penetrate the flowing stillness of his own soul.

His peace was not fleeting or erratic, but constant. Even his moments of magnificent indignation and powerful righteous wrath did not penetrate his inner peace.

In our world of tension and ragged-edged nerves, books by the million are sold which suggest theories, suggestions, and techniques for achieving calmness. Yet the only pure example is Christ, and the study of his life lays out the blueprint:

1. Live a simple life, uncluttered by too many "things,"
2. Pray always,
3. Love (the absence of fear) (1 John 4:16-18), and
4. Prepare.

The Lord Jesus Christ is not only the total example of peace: he is the source, the dispenser, the spirit through which our *own* calmness can be gained.

WEEK **44** PATIENCE

Nothing is more destructive of the peace and the calm previously discussed than impatience. The clear, light window of tranquility can be shattered in an instant by the hard, dark stone of impatience.

Peace is preserved only as patience persists. Christ is the incredibly supreme example here because no one has ever had more excuse for impatience, yet no one has ever been more totally free from it.

Consider how impatient (in fact, *impatience* is too mild a word) one would normally become:

—when his finest gifts are rejected by those to whom they are given;

89

—when his closest friends misunderstand his most important words;

—when those who seem loyal prove disloyal;

—when people forget, in a matter of days, miracles the like of which they have never before seen;

—when he gives all and has little or nothing returned;

—when he is denied by the man he has chosen to lead his organization.

We have all felt intolerance and impatience when our children, our friends, or anyone, for that matter, simply cannot understand or do something that to us is so easy or obvious.

The Master was above and somehow far beyond impatience. His spirit and peace were so deep that surface irritations were simply overpowered and engulfed by his calm.

He was like the perfect big brother who loves his little sister so totally that he helps her up each time she stumbles, wipes her eyes, encourages her—with the thought of irritation or impatience never crossing his mind.

Because of the Master's complete love, there was always a definite and clear line between his concerned, anxious desire for people to understand and any sign of impatience. When Philip missed a point about Christ's sameness with the Father, He said, "Have I been so long time with you, and yet hast thou not known me, Philip?" (John 14:9), but no doubt it was said with deep concern and love, not with ridicule or impatience. Even with the doubting Thomas there was no hint of impatience in the reply, "Be not faithless, but believing" (John 20:27).

To the Lord, humble sinners were to be helped and loved. When his indignation broke forth, it sprang not from impatience with those needing help, but as a powerful combat against Satan's evil and hypocrisy which he saw as the vulture waiting to destroy those who had fallen from the nest.

Today, perhaps one of the greatest illustrations of this quality of the Lord is his patience with our impatience.

MONTH 12

HIS BALANCE

"Be ye therefore perfect"

WEEK 45 *HARMONY OF "OPPOSITES"*

Christ attained (and exemplified) perfection in *every* facet, in every shade of life. He is the white, perfect light which gathers and includes every color of every spectrum in the rainbow.

His life stands as the ultimate example of *all* good traits—even those that, at first, seem to us to be opposites of each other:

> confidence/humility
> conviction/sympathy
> stern standards/tolerance
> susceptibility of grief/deep joy
> ambition/interest in ordinary persons
> self-culture and development/self-denial
> self-devotion/other-devotion
> commitment to a cause/patience, freedom from anxiety
> compassion/righteous indignation

It is truly amazing to ponder that list and to realize that Christ *combined* them, perfected the "opposites" simultaneously. He was completely confident, yet completely humble (see Week 41). He had maximum strength (see Month 3), yet maximum sensitivity (see Month 4). The list goes on and on.

There is greatness in balance, and balance is often the result of two great moral forces, each pulling in opposite directions. Even the earth we live on is held in place by centripetal gravity (holding in) and centrifugal force (holding out).

Danger lurks when one character trait overpowers its opposite. Conviction without sympathy makes the bigot. Liberality without positive conviction of truth leads to thoughtless toleration. Compassion without indignation produces the holy man of the East who peacefully meditates while children around him starve.

Balance is everywhere in the Lord's teaching. He didn't say "love others and not yourself". He said love others *as* yourself (see Matthew 19:19), love yourself *and* love others. He wants us to seek the best for ourselves *and* for others. The concept of "and" was important to Christ. He didn't want us to develop one good trait at the expense of another. He wanted *both*, for each of us.

He said, "For *their* sakes I sanctify myself" (John 17:19). Is he saying that he made himself good so that he could help others make themselves good? To Christ, the sin of selfishness had to do not so much with caring about oneself as with not caring about others.

Christ epitomized perfection not only in the "masculine qualities" of strength and leadership, but also in the "feminine qualities" of sensitivity, loyalty, tenderness, devotion.

He is the ultimate example of the assets of youth—delight, adventure, and freshness—but he is also the ultimate example of the assets of age—wisdom and consistency.

He is the ultimate in "Western virtues"—practicality and *action*-orientation—but also in "Eastern qualities"—meditation and *thought*-orientation.

Jesus Christ is the model for *all* good, and the example for *all* people, of any age, of any sex, of any time.

Tao, who lived six hundred years before Christ and who created the philosophy followed by hundreds of millions of Taoists today, taught that all things were held in check by two great opposing balancing forces: the yin and the yang. He grouped all opposing forces into these categories—the warm and the cold, the masculine and the feminine, the old and the young. He indicated that if there should ever appear on the earth a being who possessed all the qualities of the yin and all the qualities of the yang, that being would be God.

Again, six hundred years after Tao's profound prescription came Jesus Christ.

WEEK 46 "IN THE WORLD BUT NOT OF THE WORLD"

We often hear the admonition "Be in the world but not of the world." We assume that it is a warning, that it means we should stay apart—isolate ourselves from evil, buffer ourselves and to stand far aside from the problems and turmoil of the world.

Perhaps the statement should be viewed instead as two clear admonitions:

1. Be *in*, be part of, your world so you can *help* and *serve*.

2. Be not *of* the world in terms of its evil and its improper priorities.

Christ "came *into* the world." It might be argued that he didn't have to come, that he could have kept apart in the heavenly realms of righteousness and watched from a safe distance, but he did not. He came upon the world—and he was not only *on* it, he was *in* it. He lived *in* every part of it: the wicked part, the hypocritical part, the pious part.

Some were not comfortable about some of the places he went to. They "warned" him, they urged him to leave. He told them that a physician did not come to cure those who were well. He walked into the scorned publican's house and later made the man an apostle. He walked through the despised Samaria. He showed by his life his love for all. He told his apostles (then *and* now) to go into *all* the world and teach the gospel to *every* creature (see Mark 16:15).

Christ was *in* the world: in the peasant's world, the learned Pharisee's world, the Roman world, the worlds of all men. Through his comprehension of the principle that "right has more power than wrong," he was able to move in any circle, always lifting others up: never himself descending or being pulled down. How he must worry today about those who stay aloof from the "unworthy" when they might help to pull them up!

No one has ever been more "in the world" than Christ,

for he cared for every person and every thing, even to the point of descending beneath them all (see D&C 88:6). But no one has ever been less "of the world," for Christ's desires were never for the things "that moth and rust doth corrupt."

Christ was so caught up in lifting the world up that *it* could never pull him down. Could it not be so with us if we followed him, followed *his way* of being in the world but not of the world?

WEEK **47** CONGRUENCE

Congruence is broadly defined as internal and external consistency—being honest with one's self and honest with others. Any lack of internal or external honesty is a weakening factor—a darkening, eye-dropping loss of self. Almost every mortal lacks at least a degree of congruence, because virtually no mortal lives exactly as he knows he should, exactly as he would tell others to live.

Part of Christ's incomparable personal magnetism and power came from his *total* congruence. He taught what he was. He was what he taught. He said what he felt. He felt what he said.

Many men understand that power that comes from saying: "What you see is what you get. I may not be perfect, but I am genuine. I am real. I do not pretend to be anything that I'm not." Imagine for a moment the strength that would lie in being able to say (as Christ did): "I am truth. I am the example for all. Come, follow me."

The purpose of Christ's life was to bear witness of the truth (see John 18:37), the kind of pure truth that frees men's minds from ignorance and error (see John 8:32). His strongest rebukes were directed toward the dishonesty of hypocrites (see Matthew 15:7-9; Isaiah 29:13-15). His standard of honesty was total.

He demanded honesty not only in words and deeds, but in the *motives* behind the words and deeds. He was not pleased when the right things were done for the wrong reasons—including fasting (see Matthew 6:16-18), prayer (see Matthew 6:5-6), and service (see Matthew 6:1-4). Another definition of congruence, then, would be doing the right things for the right reasons.

Christ knew and taught that nothing can ever be right in a man's life if he is not sincere. Some lives look better outside than inside. We may compare such lives to a large paste diamond—they win admiration from others but are secretly despised by those that live them. Christ's congruence gave him the one things more prized than the respect of others: the respect of self. Trying to win the approval of others can lead to insincerity unless the deeper motive is to be worthy of God's love and to win *self*-respect. The real secret lies deep within the heart (see Matthew 15:19-20, Luke 16:15).

Christ's congruence gave his life a *consistency* which allowed Him to "do always those things that please [God]" (John 8:29), and which caused his Father to say, on virtually every recorded instance when man has heard him speak: "This is my Beloved Son, in whom I am well pleased."

To win that "in whom I am well pleased" stamp of approval is the ultimate goal of every Christian life. Congruence is a vital key to that goal. It is the kind of total honesty that the Savior consistently displayed.

WEEK 48 *PERFECTION*

Christ's perfection has been referred to by millions—notably by Paul ("holy, harmless, undefiled"; Hebrews 7:26), John ("no unrighteousness is in him"; John 7:18), and Peter ("without blemish"; 1 Peter 1:19).

The most important person who has called Christ perfect

is Christ himself (see 3 Nephi 12:48) because his evaluation is more discerning than ours and because his definition of "perfect" is far more demanding.

To ponder Christ's perfection is to ponder the unponderable. Christ was perfect not only in the sense that he never *committed* a wrong, but in the almost mind-boggling sense that he never omitted a right, never failed to help one in need, never failed to speak needed truth, never failed to be humble, to pray, to give all credit and glory to God.

Perfection is the outward symptom of the inward divinity, the factor that sets Christ apart and far above all other leaders of all other times. Among the founders of other religions, other philosophies (indeed, among all other great leaders the world has ever known) are none who, like Christ, achieved perfection in this life.

Mere men, as they grow and develop and learn and as they gain righteousness, become ever more aware of their faults, their weaknesses. Thus the greater their stature becomes, the more they recognize their imperfections and the more they are able to *contrast* themselves with this world's single perfect life—the life of a man whose development gradually revealed his perfection rather than his imperfection.

The Lord's perfection came not in the absence of temptation, but through overcoming the greatest temptations. We know he was tempted "in all points, like as we are" (Hebrews 4:15) and that he "descended below all things" (D&C 88:6):

3

POSTSCRIPT

What About Next Year?

There are 112 chapters in scripture that directly record our Lord's ministry on this earth (the four Gospels and chapters 8-30 of 3 Nephi).

Try reading a few pages each Sunday before you partake of the sacrament. Don't just *read*—read specifically to *know* the Lord. Pause after each verse to ask your own mind and the Holy Spirit's mind, "What does that verse tell me about Jesus? about his character? his personality? his love?

Perhaps the format of this book can be the format for marginal notes in your scriptures (my scripture margins are covered with the words *loyalty, sensitivity, strength, calmness, perfection*, and so on).

There are many beneficial ways to read scripture. You can read to look for history, for doctrine, for counsel; but try reading 112 chapters for clues to Christ's character, for principles of his personality.

A few pages each Sunday before the sacrament will provide another small step in the goal of life and the joy of life: coming to know the Lord Jesus Christ.

As you close the cover, reflect on the fact that the key factor separating the inheritors of the celestial and terrestrial glories is valiance in the testimony of Jesus (see D&C 76).

Book designed by Michael Clane Graves
Composed by University Services, Inc.
in Times Roman with display lines in
Futura Medium and Futura Medium Italic
Printed by Publishers Press
on 60# Simpson Antique
Bound by Mountain States Bindery
in Sturdetan "40034" Tropical Green, Buckram Finish